Barb—
I am so
very excited to
see you again.
Thank you for
years
support!
Melanie

The
RISE & FALL
of a
MOMOCRACY

Dear I am so excited to

The
RISE & FALL
of a
MOMOCRACY

MELANIE DANKE

Plumb Tuckered Books
4420 17th Avenue South
Minneapolis, MN 55407

For more information, visit www.plumbtuckeredout.com
or email melanie@plumbtuckeredout.com

ISBN: 978-0-9970916-0-1

Printed in the United States of America

First Edition

This book is dedicated to Hattie, Sam, Besso, Tigi, and Miki—I joke around, but really, I work every day to be worthy of you. Where would I possibly be without such supportive, funny, and unbelievably messy cheerleaders? I love you.

And to Kirk, because you always said I could.

CONTENTS

In the Beginning, There Was Cosmo

never meant to have so many children. In truth, I never thought I'd have any. Even though I earned the bulk of my junior high school Banana Taffy and roller rink money babysitting, I never considered myself particularly maternal. Oh, sure, watching the neighborhood rug rats let me rake in the then princely sum of one dollar an hour, but I still couldn't muster much enthusiasm for the younger crowd. (Oh, what I wouldn't give for twenty-four extra bucks a day now; I could probably afford to purchase my wine in actual bottles.)

Near as I could figure, motherhood was for suckers, and I promised myself that I would never get tied down. I had a brilliant future ahead of me, one that involved a big city apartment with a view of the skyline and acres of white carpeting. (In those days, I got my decorating tips from the television show *Dynasty*. Fashion tips, too. You should have seen the size of my shoulder pads.) As I saw it, I was destined to be the youngest ever editor of *Cosmopolitan* magazine and fully expected I would be far too busy attending fashion galas and canoodling with male models to sire the next generation.

I had heard somewhere that the best surprises came in little blue boxes labeled "Tiffany's," so imagine my surprise when, midway through my slacker twenties, I learned that some surprises show up as little baby girls who look, hilariously, an awful lot like Winston Churchill. From the moment our eldest daughter arrived, the die was cast. She was barely toddling about on her own, when I started lobbying a somewhat reluctant Hubby for our next production, *Baby: The Sequel* (tag line: "This time it's on purpose.").

Two babies in, we couldn't believe what great parents we were. We were happy, the kids were healthy, and we hardly ever dropped them. Clearly, we owed it to ourselves, nay, our world, to raise more humans. But how?

I was more than happy to forgo the blessed miracle of birth, and Hubby didn't argue. To this day when speaking of my two labors, he uses the hushed tone of someone who has witnessed a particularly disturbing accident. In both instances, I was ineffectually shushed by maternity ward nurses for swearing nonstop at the top of my lungs for hours until they broke down and gave me the mother effing epidural already. (An actual quote by one of my nurses: "Stop it! You are scaring the other mothers!")

That's how we came to adopt our three youngest children: twin sisters and their little brother from Ethiopia.

So, here I sit, far from *Cosmo.* I'm married to a man whose childhood dream was to own a station wagon and am surrounded by these children who rip through the house like five happy little wrecking balls, only louder and with more destruction. I couldn't have landed farther from the life I promised myself. No fancy job, no white carpet, no galas . . .

Although, sometimes, there is canoodling, very careful canoodling. Because five kids is a lot. But, six? That would be *crazy.*

Where Is All My Stuff?

Do you know what the greatest problem is once you bring children into your family? It's not the noise, or the ungodly mess, or the irreversible aging that comes from lack of sleep. It's not even the fact that your stomach muscles have fallen like a snapped rubber band and you have neither the time nor the energy to do a thing about it.

The problem is that once children have been steeped in the intimacy of a family, once they have been assured of the unbroken continuity of your love, you will never be able to convince them to leave your stuff alone.

My kids think everything that is mine is theirs, which is so patently untrue. It is, perhaps, the most infuriating thing about parenthood.

Listen to me, my children. You have my undying love and unconditional support, but if I find any of you in my dresser again, I will take all of your favorite Christmas gifts and bury them in the backyard.

Go ahead. See if I'm kidding.

My earrings, my clothing, my hidden stash of chocolate are all, apparently, up for grabs. My iPod, should I be lucky enough to find it, lies orphaned, sans headphones, on the coffee table. I haven't seen a grown-up pair of scissors for years. All my pens have disappeared, my awesome potato peeler (as seen on TV) turned up in the compost pile, and someone buried my garlic press in the garden. Why, Lord, why?

I don't ask for much. All that I require for exquisite, eternal happiness is the September issue of *Vogue* magazine, a never-ending supply of fun-sized Snickers bars, and for my stuff to remain exactly where I left it. I have enough trouble attempting to remember where everything is without five little minions using my possessions in an impromptu game of "Capture the Flag."

You, my children, may find it hilarious to watch Mommy's face turn from pink to red to mottled purple, but there is nothing funny about a brain aneurysm. Take one more thing, and you better hope that you remember where you left my cell phone, because someone is going to need to call 911.

And worse than all that is the fact that this disease—the "can't-keep-their-fingers-off-it-itis"—is apparently transferable. It started with Miss Teen Wonder, the first born fruit of my loins, and has spread slowly but surely to infect all of our children, biological or no. Every last one of them shows symptoms, and, God help me, it appears that they are carriers. I'm no doctor, but I think they are spreading this disease to their friends.

Don't believe me? I currently lack a fall jacket because not even my daughter, but my daughter's *best friend* is wearing it.

Somebody better find that phone.

At times like these, I will pause for a moment and consider why I decided to have kids in the first place.

I have no idea.

It wasn't really a well-thought-out decision. It was more of an absence of doubt. If you know me well at all, you know that I expend an awful lot of energy worrying about the choices I make. Should I or shouldn't I? Would it be better to do this or that? I spend an inordinate amount of what could be enjoyable leisure time wringing my hands and assuming the "what have I done?" posture (hand rubbing forehead, eyes closed, head bowed over a stress-relieving dessert or a glass of wine or preferably both). But when it came to whether or not to expand our family, I had absolute clarity.

Of course. Bring it.

There was no sort of logical thought process involved, which was darn lucky for my kids. Logic doesn't play into this decision well at all. *Logically*, if someone asked if you'd consider bringing a gaggle of screeching little vandals into your home, you'd think twice. Suppose this person then told you that, furthermore, they are going to be a daily presence for the next several decades of your life. They are going to eat your food; consume the bulk of your resources, time, energy, and youth; and will repay you by making boneheaded decisions that threaten their future, if not their very lives. (Such as sketchy boyfriends, poor school performance, or plywood bike ramps in the alley.) *Logically*, you should tell the person proposing this clearly insane idea to jump in the lake, but emotionally . . .

That's where children get you. They are miracles really. And, at least for me, they extend that glow to the world around them. Even when I am fixing to, in the words of another mom, twist their heads clean off, I am often inwardly marveling at their beauty. Honestly, I am so grateful that I get to be their mom. And when they are driving me crazy? That's when I'm grateful for wine. See how it all works out?

There are other upsides to sharing your life with children, such as personal growth. You may not see it now, since I look like a crazy person, unkempt and on the edge of a serious public meltdown, but give me a few years and you won't even recognize me. I'm going to be great, and once I make it through these next few years, I'm going to be so very mellow. Stop laughing, it is totally true. Even as I write this, the stress from all the begging, whining, and maddeningly unending noise is exerting the kind of pressure that can turn this little old lump of coal into a diamond. What could possibly be more stressful than day-to-day life with five children all begging for money, iPods, and sleepovers, while simultaneously breaking everything you have given them and leaving the pieces scattered throughout the house?

And speaking of the house, mine is going to be so clean when these rug rats finally ship out of here. Currently, I spend a boatload of energy trying to keep the place in line, and it still is one sick day away from an episode of *Hoarders*. God, I can only dream of how fabulous this place will look when all my stuff remains exactly where I put it, when we use fewer than twenty-one glasses a day, and when the laundry pile no longer dwarfs my five-foot seven-inch tall body. I may even have energy for dusting (but I wouldn't go all crazy about it).

There are other, less obvious, gains. For example, if the kids have their way, all of them would have lessons or play dates or some form of activity every blessed night. Even with our tight-fisted hold on our schedule and our refusal to let anyone join more than two—TWO—extracurriculars, scheduling still is a nightmare. Hence, I have learned to fight my Midwestern compulsion to avoid "being a bother" at any costs and accept help when offered.

For example, Miss Teen Wonder enjoys periodically attending a youth group. Problem: It isn't anywhere in our neighborhood. No, it has to be held more than half an hour away and on a weeknight, besides. Plus, the darn thing lasts two hours. That means I have nothing to do but to sit and stare out the window of the minivan because this place is in Nowheresville, man. I know it's hard to believe, given the seeming unbroken chain of coffee shops, SuperTargets, and fast-food restaurants that litter most areas of our modern landscape, but there is nothing, absolutely nothing, near this group's meeting place. Not a Barnes and Noble to be found. If there was only something I could productively be doing at that time, I probably wouldn't kick at all. Okay, I would, but less often and less strenuously.

But suggest to the princess that you don't want to waste an evening twiddling your thumbs while your four other children are at home unsupervised, and she quickly morphs from princess to drama queen, moaning about her need to "feed her soul," to which I reply that, frankly, I'd rather she clean her room. This, while hilarious, does not lead to one of our better mother-daughter moments.

It took me two years, *two years*, to finally break down and let one of the youth leaders drive her home. Because I am an idiot, apparently.

But an idiot who learns. From now on if you want to drive one of my kids somewhere, *anywhere*, thank you. Thank you and God bless you. You have preserved my tenuous sanity for one more day, and my husband, for one, couldn't be happier about it. I'd call you and thank you, but I can't seem to find the phone.

Meet the Cast and Crew

It occurs to me that it would probably be helpful to know a little bit about the folks I am most certainly going to complain high and low about. It will make it ever so much easier to understand that none of this is my fault, so help me God.

Hubby

All in all, he's a decent guy. I met him through a roommate, who invited him to a brunch we were hosting due to the great fortune of having discovered that the previous tenants had left a large, uncut slab of bacon in the freezer. Because his mother had raised him well, Hubby called the next morning and asked if there was anything we needed. My roommate held the phone at arm's length and repeated the question, loudly. Thus, the very first words my future beloved heard me speak were: "Toilet paper."

Enchanting.

Despite the fact that my ex-boyfriend was at the brunch and I was half out of my mind with the effort of affecting a cheerful noncha-lance, Hubby managed to make an impression. It helped that he was so darn tall, six four, in fact. Wearing a pushed back fedora, he was slim as a bean pole with striking blue eyes and an easy grin. Irresistible. A mere ten minutes after he left, my roommate and I were in a huddle, already plotting the next meeting. Three months later, we were engaged. He never really stood a chance.

Now he's stuck with me. Sucker. He's kind, extremely intelligent, and generous in his affection for the people around him. If you ask, he sometimes will list one of his greatest assets as the ability to get along with difficult people. This is usually followed with a theatrical sideways glance in my direction—a move that would normally warrant a certain amount of justifiable bodily harm, if he didn't immediately follow it up with a laugh I happen to find endearing.

Like everyone, he has his negatives. Because he is so good natured, people entirely miss how completely pig-headed he can be. After twenty-three years, I am intimately acquainted with the tight-lipped smile and slight nod of the head that means whatever I just said has been, without fanfare, summarily rejected. Also, he still thinks he will one day convince me to let him raise chickens in our backyard. So, maybe he's not so intelligent. He is infuriatingly sanguine about the state of our pitiful kitchen and has a dislike of Christmas that I'm pretty sure is going to keep him out of heaven.

Still, he is a really, really good dad. He doesn't mind that I swear, which I do constantly, or drink wine, which I also do constantly. He tolerates my addiction to SuperTarget and loves me even though the voice I use to impersonate him when telling stories to my sister is not, in the strictest sense, complementary.

Miss Teen Wonder (Hattie)

Our firstborn and, likely as not, the reason for my upcoming heart attack, she is funny, charming, and infuriatingly underachieving. Every now and again, I remember the day my mother, exasperated beyond belief with her own firstborn daughter, pointed a finger at me and said, "Just you wait. One day you will have a daughter. Just. Like. You." At the time, I told her I thought it sounded wonderful. Now, it sounds like karma biting me in the butt.

One Sunday Miss Teen Wonder thought I was mad at her and

sent me an unbroken string of Internet cat pictures until I begged her to stop. Her career goal is to be "a mermaid," but she's going to have problems finding a college for that. If she had spent half as much time studying for her ACTs as she has perfecting her cat-eye eyeliner technique, she could have gotten a full scholarship to any university in the country, perhaps the world. She wears cute retro dresses but will also make her belly button "talk" to you. She is talkative and also remarkably open with me. On the surface, that sounds great, but it often just causes me to put my head on the table and lament our apparent lapses of parental vigilance.

SammyJ

Our eldest son is a carbon copy of his father but better because I grew him myself. I remember watching him sleep one night, when he was very young, and turning to Hubby and saying, "If you, Sammy, and I are ever in a fire and I only can save one of you. . . . Well, I love you and all, but good luck to you. I'm telling you now because I just don't want there to be any unpleasant surprises. Other than the fire, I mean."

I was certain I would never have sons. Little boys were completely incomprehensible to me, so much so that I doubted my body was capable of producing one. It would have been, I thought, like a panda giving birth to a hyena. Once, when I was pregnant with his sister, I went for a walk and saw two brothers standing in their backyard. They had each collected a largish pile of rocks and had commenced a game, which, as near as I could tell, consisted of taking turns standing still while the other chucked rocks at them. They were stoning each other for fun. My boys like to play, "Come at me, Bro'," which is pretty much what it sounds like. My point is: what the hell?

I still don't know why boys do the things they do. I cannot predict a single thing related to their behavior based on my female logic. However, it's not as terrible as I had assumed it would be. It is not just aggression that plays out in their physicality but also their affections. When little boys feel affectionate, they will flat out knock you down, scramble up your inert form, and plant their little sneakers on your stomach, hand, and face because, you know, LOVE. One of SammyJ's elementary school friends had a little sister with Down syndrome, and they *loved* her. They would hug her, kiss her, give her piggyback rides, dance with her to whatever song she wanted, or let her ride them like Shetland ponies. It was completely disarming to see that much love pouring out of their little bodies. Who knew?

Nowadays, in high school, SammyJ is still charming the ladies. He is terribly tight-lipped about everything. It's as if he is a Russian spy at a U.N. cocktail party—best not say anything for fear he might inadvertently give up the location of their secret, offshore military base. He is on the cross-country team, the ski team, and the track team. He hangs with the seniors and is cool in a way that I never was. "I know what you're up to!" I say, wagging my finger at him, but I don't. I have no idea. He is as much a mystery to me as he ever was, but I'd still grab him in a fire. Sorry, hon.

Double Trouble a.k.a. the Twins (Besso and Tigist)

Everyone knows that you shouldn't treat twins as a single entity, but really, it is difficult when they are, for all intents and purposes, inseparable. Not that they are the same. *Au contraire.* From the first moment we met them, ten years ago in Ethiopia, they have displayed polar opposite traits. However, rather than this setting them apart, it feels like two sides of one coin.

Besso is more outgoing, with a raucous laugh and an unflagging enthusiasm. When we met with their biological family a few years ago, they told the story of a two-year-old Besso, who was instructed to stay in the yard and to stop wandering around the town. She then insisted on standing like a sentry at the door to the gate and at the first hint of approaching footsteps, she would fling open the door and invite whomever was passing to "Come in! Come in!" Years later, Besso and her two biological siblings would stand, blocking the sidewalk whenever pedestrians would appear outside our house in Minneapolis, peppering them with inquiries, requests, and the offer to sing them a song—or four. We finally took pity on our neighbors and instituted a strong "three-question" rule. After the third question, our children had to stand aside and let folks pass. (It was an unpopular rule.) Despite her diminutive height (four feet ten inches, the same as her sister), Besso is sturdy and strong and has an innate sense of her body. First cartwheel? Nailed it. First dive? Perfect. However, she abhors competition and, rather than risk coming in second, will fling her body to the ground in a comical pratfall worthy of Charlie Chaplin.

Not so, her sister. Tigist is more self-contained, living her life as a never-ending telenovella running continuously in her head and which she narrates softly to herself. I suspect this tendency is due to her extremely poor eyesight. I imagine that when she was young, in lieu of visual stimulation, she became quite good at constructing whole worlds in her head. She is also quietly, but fiercely, competitive. Her current goals: Win *American Idol* at sixteen and become an Olympic sprinter. One time, she heard me discussing my marathon mile-per-minute pace with Hubby and decided to razz me about it.

"Hey," I said indignantly, "You may be faster, but I can go longer. I just ran for almost five hours."

She shot me a look of disdain and replied, "I could, too, if I ran that slow."

She didn't give me a head wag and a finger snap, but it was definitely implied.

Which brings us to . . .

Little Man (Miki)

I say this with all the love in a mother's heart—this child is going to be the death of me. So effortlessly smart. So beautiful. So engaging. So high strung. It's like trying to parent a champion racehorse. From the beginning, Little Man screamed if I came anywhere near him, as if I were covertly jabbing him with red-hot pokers. He loved Hubby on sight; five minutes after our introductions in Ethiopia, he was cooing "Baba!" ("Daddy!") and lifting his sweet little arms to be picked up. One day in Ethiopia, Hubby had to leave for an afternoon to find a bank and cash some traveler's checks. Little Man screamed so hard and unceasingly that the care center staff clustered around our room, ears to the door, certain I was torturing him. Had we an interpreter capable of infant-to-English translation, I'm pretty sure we would have confirmed that the idea Little Man was trying to convey was, "This woman is NOT THE BOSS OF ME!"

If it is true that the people we have the greatest conflict with are those from whom we learn the most, Little Man has been my greatest teacher. Here is an abbreviated list of what I have learned so far:

1. You cannot force a person to do a single thing. Sure, you can try to stack the deck in your favor, so that the person's choice comes down to: do what I want or never see your iPod/TV/ the sunrise ever again, but it will be a hollow victory.

2. Box wine does the job just as well as bottled and is cheaper, too.

3. Usually, the child you are in conflict with is the one that is most like you.

4. That last one really blows.

5. Arguing is not the same as not loving. If I didn't desperately love these kids, I would let them do whatever the hell they wanted. I am too tired to give one rat's patootie about the actions of people I couldn't care less about. As it is, they are too precious and too full of potential for me to let them grow up to be as stubborn and undisciplined as, well, their mother (see #3 above).

You should also know that Little Man is unbelievably charming. In our neighborhood, they call him The Mayor. He knows every man, woman, and child for a four-block radius. He knows who is moving and where to. He knows who is getting a new job or another puppy. The reason he knows is because he is funny and engaging. He has great conversational skills and is truly interested in whatever the person is saying.

I work about a twenty-minute drive from home. One night, while ringing up an order, I discovered that the customer and I shared the same zip code. In fact, the customer had recently moved into a house one block away from ours.

"Oh, you know my son then," I said.

"Uh, no," he replied skeptically.

I raised an eyebrow. "Really? African American kid? Eleven years old? Loves to talk?"

"Oh, MIKI," he said.

Damn right, The Mayor.

I'm No Expert, But . . .

Two things you should know about my mother are: she is exceedingly private, and she hates to be pinned down. Writing anything about her at all violates both of these rules, so there is a good chance I'm about to get into big, big trouble. Still . . .

One of my favorite stories about my mother starts with me coming to her with a rash.

"What do you think this is?" I asked.

Throwing the barest of glances my way, she replied nonchalantly, "Probably leprosy."

As if first grade wasn't challenging enough.

Although this seemed a notable development to my young mind, Mom's reaction was shockingly blasé. "These things happen," she seemed to be saying and so I took my cue from her. I wandered through my days, without any obvious distress, but every night, I did a total body scan. I knew leprosy was contagious, and I was waiting for that first toe or finger to fall off, at which point my plan was to hitch a ride to Hawaii to join a leper colony in order to spare my family a similar fate. I remember being concerned about how I, at a mere six years of age, was going to find a job to support myself, and so, I put a great amount of effort into preparing a short speech of introduction. I hoped that, should I be lucky enough to find a nice leper family, I would prove so winsome and charming that they would agree to care for me on the spot.

Eventually, the rash went away. Still years away from really grasping the concept of sarcasm, I marveled at the wild inaccuracy of my mom's diagnosis.

"Good thing she's not a doctor!" I told myself cheerfully and got on with my busy schedule of pilfering Hostess cupcakes to use as rations while I pretended to be lost in the woods behind my house.

I love this story. I love even more that Mom had no idea how seriously I took her comment. I love that apparently I recovered sufficiently to go on to torment my own children.

One time, when Miss Teen Wonder was young, we were camping and news came that a tornado had been seen in the area.

"Mom, where will we go if a tornado touches down in the campground?" she asked worriedly.

"Up," I replied, not at all unreasonably.

Although she points to this as evidence that I am not the paragon of motherhood that she had hoped I would be, I see it as a fine example of the strength of tradition. A certain macabre sense of humor runs straight through my mom's bloodline and into my brother, my sister, and me. God willing, I've passed it on to my kids as well. I hope so. It's the only inheritance they are likely to receive.

Mom's sometimes off-beat sense of humor is balanced by her dedication to good manners. I've had the privilege of being "raised right." If I go into a nice restaurant and see a fellow diner still wearing his baseball cap, the only thing keeping me pinned to my seat upon noticing this breach of manners is the knowledge that stomping to his table, snatching the cap from his head, and setting it, pointedly, on the seat beside him would make a scene, an even worse transgression. I will, however, glower at him throughout the meal and attempt to send the offending hat flying from his head with the power of my mind, but that isn't nearly as effective as I would like.

Recently, my twin daughters and I were standing outside a movie theater, waiting for Hubby to arrive. We witnessed a girl, maybe fifteen years old, stomp across the street, mid-block, leaving her two elderly grandparents struggling to keep up. She snapped at them disrespectfully when they suggested that they use the crosswalk, and when her mother appeared with the car, she took off at a rapid clip, offering no arm for support to her grandparents. Then, she did the unimaginable. She yanked open the front passenger door—the front door!—and huffed her way into the car. My jaw actually dropped. First off, the FRONT SEAT? When I was a child, we observed a strict automotive hierarchy—in the presence of any adult, children were to sit in the back, in the middle, with their feet on the hump, and count themselves lucky they even got that.

Tigist turned to me, her face mirroring my own indignation, and said, "That girl is terrible."

"Yes," I agreed and we shook our heads in unison. The only reason my kids would never, ever engage in similar behavior is that my mother never, ever would allow me to, either. She fought valiantly to pound into our skulls the ideas of respect and courtesy. Watching that girl's behavior made me think that maybe "You are not the most important person in the room" is a lesson we need to revisit as a society. At the risk of sounding like a total curmudgeon, let me tell you what is wrong with the youth of today.

Parents. Parents are what is wrong with the youth of today.

Kids have been the same throughout history—miniature people lacking skills, motor control, and table manners and possessing a super-human capacity to resist all attempts to civilize them. Civilizing the next generation—that's our job, isn't it? We're supposed to give them the skills to get along in the world and to be happy and successful—at least successful enough that when they are finally adults, we can move in with them, and not vice versa.

Traditionally, this happens by providing our children with a model to aspire to. We display a veneration for our elders, saying to our children in our words and actions that this is what they should strive for: to live a long life of competence, kindness, sacrifice, and hard work. Maybe when you know something you can sit in the front seat, goddammit, but until then, all the places of honor—the front seat, the head of the table, and the good recliner—are for the grown-ups.

In the past, children were rightfully low on the totem pole and treated like the vaguely amusing hobos they were—they had no job and no real responsibility. Any work parents managed to wring out of their children, via the half-assed completion of chores, was achieved through a combination of tears and threats, usually on both sides. Any parent knows that it requires far more effort and time to coerce a child to complete a task than it does simply to do it yourself. But that is how children learn, by badgering them relentlessly until they reluctantly and resentfully accomplish the work. This is what we call "success." And if we are lucky, the resulting stress-induced aneurysm happens decades later, when our hard work has borne fruit and our children can afford to give us the very best of nursing home care.

Somehow, for many people, this has gotten turned around. This new "children first" culture has me baffled. That we should defer in all things to the least capable members of our society just boggles my mind. Children are inherently selfish and whim-driven. They are incapable of grasping the concept of delayed gratification or setting aside their desires for a greater good. That joyful enthusiasm that bubbles unbidden from them? That is not due to an innate wisdom; it is because they *do not have a job.* Trust me, if I didn't have to go to work, or provide, prepare, and serve meals, or waste my precious resources on disappointingly dull services such as oil changes and orthodontist appointments, I would be deliriously happy, too. Every minute of every day.

Though I have been gainfully employed for thirty-plus years, I have never mustered up any enthusiasm for the life of a working stiff. The other day Hubby told me that I "was really well suited to being a writer." I can't, for the life of me, take that as an entirely complimentary statement. What he probably meant is that he sees a marked difference in my enthusiasm and general zest for life when I have free days dedicated solely to writing. What I *hear* is: "You are really well suited to any job you can do in your pajamas, on the couch, a mere arm's length from an obscene amount of peanut butter toast and that involves long stretches of staring out the window, because you are *thinking*, dangnabbit!"

True or not, this ideal of easy labor runs counter to my internal, Midwestern value of hard work. The tension between the two has always been somewhat of a struggle for me. I think if you know me, you know that I've always worked hard. I've had one, sometimes two jobs at a time since I was fifteen years old, and I've tried hard to excel at all of them.

What fewer people know is that, on the inside, having to work for a living has always made me weep like an exiled Russian princess told she has to wash her own teacup. Bitter, bitter tears. It feels like karmic payback, like maybe in a past life I ran a puppy mill or burned witches. Maybe I was Imelda Marcos or a lumber baron. If my parents hadn't instilled in me the idea that, yes, Virginia, you really, really have to work for a living, I don't know where I'd be. I lack the fundamental computer programming skills of a hacker, which is the only under-the-table endeavor I can envision that would provide the life to which I'd like to become accustomed.

Which brings me to technology. Despite the inherent definition, technology is nothing new, at least, not in how parents and kids deal with it. I once was in a class where we were discussing the translations of ancient Greek texts. I kid you not, more than one passage turned out to be a diatribe about kids and their new-fangled ways. Yes, thousands of years ago, parents were longing for "the good old days" and lamenting the ruination of the youth. Probably, we will one day discover cave paintings whose mysterious symbols turn out to say, "Ugh. Kids and their wheels, am I right?"

When I glance out my front window and see a row of my kids and their friends, all sitting on the porch, companionably close, but all absorbed in their own tiny screens, it makes me want to go all Grandma Clampett and chase them off with a broom.

"Talk to each other!" I want to shout, "With your actual FACES! Look at your own cat, instead of that online one caught in a box . . . okay, that one is pretty cute . . . but still. Everything that you are looking at on your iPod happened somewhere in real life. Get out there!"

Of course, this carries absolutely no weight with them. If I were, perhaps, somehow proficient with technology, I could make a more convincing argument as to its proper place in their lives.

Technology leaves me admittedly befuddled. Thursday night, I spent the better part of the evening cussing out my failing printer and then attempting to fix it through the brilliant technique of staring gloomily at it for thirty-five minutes, pushing random bits with a pencil, and repeatedly plugging and unplugging the cord. You will be shocked to learn that this had no discernible effect on the machine.

It wouldn't have bothered me quite as much if I hadn't already been beaten down by my inability to comprehend the digital world. My understanding of social media stalled out at Facebook. I never even made it to Twitter. I cannot decipher the proper ins and outs of tweets, which are written in a language akin to Sanskrit, I believe. Yes, I *did* google "How to write a tweet," thank you very much. Also, "What the heck does this tweet say?" and "What are these stupid symbols in this tweet?" and "What the hell was wrong with email, anyway?"—none of which provided any sort of illumination.

My husband shares my technophobia, and so we ineffectively attempt to limit our children's access to electronics, convinced as we are that their iPods have turned them into ill-mannered, borderline illiterates with an addict's need for instant gratification. (Not that we are biased in any way.) Because of this, we have a strict no phone/iPod rule at the dinner table. Every so often, however, I see the kids attempt to covertly check their messages.

"No tweeting while you're eating," I'll chirp, only to be told that, "MOM, we haven't tweeted in years." Now they are "kik"-ing or "snapchatting" or something—information that is thankfully communicated to me through the age-old teen language of half-grunts and eye rolls, otherwise I'd have no idea what they are talking about.

Let me say that my inability to grasp technology troubles me deeply. I have always believed in the importance of a flexible mind. I am the first to admit that I am not the smartest person in the room. Too much of my brain is dedicated to pop culture and song lyrics and not enough to, say, world history or trade embargoes. But I have always taken pride in having a certain mental quickness. I remember things quite easily and usually have no problems immediately assimilating new concepts. Throughout my life, my thoughts have felt like a nimble, yellow ball, bouncing quickly through the rooms of my brain—until it thuds into the rigid walls of my "technological lobe" and sinks to a stop.

Dead ball on the court.

This is deeply discouraging. I am forty-six years old, an age that, in my mind, I associate with a certain competence. When my grandfather was my age, he could fix anything: tractor, phone, faucet, cracked foundation. My father is probably building a new shed somewhere, right this instant. And here I sit, morosely poking at my printer with a writing implement, profoundly resentful of the technology that has reduced me to this state.

I do not grasp the logic of how these devices work. I do not have an app for that. My default is set to "old-timey." I do my taxes with a pencil and a piece of scratch paper and largely regard the World Wide Web—the singular most powerful tool available to mankind— as mainly a receptacle for celebrity gossip and recipes.

My friends' husbands are by and large totally tech savvy. My husband would communicate through telegraph if there was anyone left who understood Morse code. So, clearly, he is no help. Every so often, Hubby will be working on some paperwork-y thing and I will hear him get up, then the opening and closing of drawers, then several moments of bad-natured huffing, and finally, the inevitable bellow, "WHERE'S the STAPLER?"

Really? Do people still make those? I literally have had no cause to use one since, oh, 1986. But there he stands, glaring at me, demanding to know where we keep ours.

"In the woodshed," I say, "next to the abacus and the loom." Together we are the worst-prepared couple to approach the technological revolution since your grandparents. The past three times we have been forced to purchase a computer, I have, perhaps hypocritically, capitalized on my children's technological prowess. I simply dumped all boxes containing keyboards, monitors, and something called an "air port" in the middle of the living room floor and told the kids to call us when it was set up. Then I retired to my bedchamber to read hieroglyphics on papyrus scrolls until supper.

They would have been within their rights to simply refuse to do it, given my frequent and lengthy soliloquies against the dangers of their growing dependence on their dang phones and tablets and whatnot. I know, too, that I am not setting a good example when they come downstairs for a glass of water late at night and find me still hunched over my own screen, following some ridiculous and meaningless thread, usually related to snarky celebrity commentary or "fashions over forty" (sigh).

"I am a cautionary tale!" I will tell the child, who is snickering, none too silently, in the darkness.

My one hope is that somehow they will adapt, as children always have, and use these new machines to create a society that is based on creativity, innovation, and human connection, despite my dire predictions. I'll be left behind, as the older generation always is, but since that's where the books and actual three-dimensional humans will be, and, of course, Hubby, I'm sure I'll be just fine.

#Isurehopeso #goodluckyoungins #toldyouso

The Shining Momocracy
on the Hill

One time, when the four youngest children were attempting to stage a coup by challenging some judgment of mine and calling for a vote, our eldest daughter decided to lay some wisdom on them.

"Guys," she said, shaking her head, "put your hands down. This isn't a democracy. It's a MOMocracy."

Oh, if only that were true.

Remember when you were a kid and you thought that being a grown-up meant that you would get to do whatever you wanted? Every day while I toiled under the oppressive yoke of my parents, I thought, "When I grow up, things are going to be different." By "different" I meant I would hardly ever have to do chores, and nobody, but nobody, would tell me what to do. Instead I grew up, got a job, had kids, and now my days are filled with an endless list of work to be done. Plus, I am surrounded by people who want nothing more than to share their dissenting opinions on every single directive I offer. If I could go back in time, I'd tell my young self to stop bellyaching and finish vacuuming the living room floor so we could spend the rest of the afternoon watching Scooby Doo and eating Suzy Qs. I never had it so good.

I am currently embroiled in a bitter battle with my eldest son. His job is to empty the various garbage containers in our home. He is *offended* by the biodegradable bags I have purchased, and even more so by my suggestion that we return to the days of simply lining the trash bins with newspaper. My motives are pure, and my concern for the environment laudable. However, as this plan of action slightly increases the possibility that one of his hands may come into direct contact with—gasp—trash, my son finds it unacceptable. You would think that in my own home I would get some say in the matter, but I don't. Or at least not without a fight.

Every meal I cook is dissected in meticulous detail by each and every member of the family. It is easier for a restaurant to get a Michelin star than it is for me to get a vote of approval from this crowd, believe me. No one likes or will wear the clothes I buy for them and good luck trying to get a single person, husband included, to follow any of the rules I've set in an attempt to keep this place from falling in around us: Little Man insists on wearing his baseball cleats around the house; everyone refuses to clean the bathtub, having decided that the shower curtain forms an impenetrable boundary that cannot be breached; and clean clothes are rarely, if ever, put away, until the stacks of folded clothes threaten to avalanche to the laundry room floor.

Also, good luck trying to get anyone else in this joint to fold laundry.

A momocracy would be so much different. So clean, so peaceful. If I were truly in charge, I have no doubt that our lives would be a utopia of gracious manners and cheerful productivity. As it stands, the opposition has taken over and is exerting its influence by staging sullen sit-down strikes and grinding forward progress to a halt.

If only they could see how wonderful our lives would be if they simply followed each and every one of my decrees. I am not a selfish despot. I wish all citizens of our fiefdom to be happy and successful. So many of my actions are based on this aim—helping them to be the very best that they can be. How could that go wrong?

Don't answer that.

I am also dedicated to a serene environment for all, if only because of my complete abhorrence for conflict. I've never grown out of the heart-thumping internal panic brought on by strife. I am a first child, far better suited to, say, undying adoration and worship, than the harsh sting of criticism and anger. Today at work I had the misfortune of dealing with an irate customer, and while I have worked diligently to temper my knee-jerk response to flee or fall possum-like to the floor, faking death or possible narcolepsy, I found the whole conversation trying at best.

I stuck it out, breathing deeply and smiling in a reassuring manner. "No problem," I said, "I'm sure we can work this out." The customer left, happily it seemed, until she called moments later to see if she had left her glasses in the shop. Our connection was bad as the phone was cutting in and out, causing our conversation to stutter forward and then grind to a halt as we both tried to talk in unison around the interference. At once I heard a loud clap and then her frustrated scream, "Shut the (blankity blank) up! You never let me (blankity blank, blank, blankity blank) talk!" which is exactly the kind of thing you say when you *think* you just hung up on someone.

I was equal parts shocked and amused. No doubt she would have been mortified if I had let it be known that I had heard her. Instead, I gently hung up the phone on my end and made the universal "cuckoo" sign to my co-workers. What? It was the most mature response I was capable of, given my delicate emotional state. Seeing the humor in the situation didn't keep my left arm from going numb, though. I kid you not; it took a full hour to get feeling all the way back to my fingertips. At what point am I going to mature sufficiently that an exchange of angry words with a random stranger does not lead to a mild cardiac event? Probably never, which is why everyone should just follow my lead and we'll all get along so much better.

The last thing I need after such trauma is anything short of complete obedience when I get home—and we all know the chances of that happening. There isn't a single Las Vegas bookie that would back that bet. I'm not giving up, though. At some point, these knuckleheads with whom I live will realize that Mother really does know best. Although, with my luck, it will probably be posthumously. What a shame that will be. To think of all the wasted years, years that we could have been enjoying flowers in every room, clean bathroom towels hanging in an orderly fashion on assigned hooks, pristine rows of sneakers in the entryway, and every Saturday, after the chores were finished, Scooby Doo reruns and Suzy Q snack cakes for everyone. It would've been glorious.

There Has to Be a Better Way

I just received a phone call at work from one of my kids.

"Mom!" he began urgently, "I forgot to tell you last week that my homeroom teacher says I'm missing a shot, and if I don't get it by tomorrow, they won't let me come to school."

Damn. I knew we needed a corkscrew at work. Also, a wet bar.

"Are you kidding me?" I said, my voice rising at least an octave. "Why didn't you tell me? Why didn't they call me?"

"They said they did. They said they contacted you on the phone and sent you a letter."

Okay, let me say this: I hate the phone. There are only four people in this world I willingly talk to and attempting to hand me the darn thing to answer it? Might as well try to get Dracula to, here, hold this crucifix for a minute.

As a result, I fully admit that there are times when messages go unanswered, but not this time. I knew for a fact that there were no messages on the machine. Besides which, I had just sorted through the huge stack of mail and paid the bills, and there was no letter from the school. How dare they spring this on me? Don't they know that people are busy? Don't they understand that we have jobs and obligations? I was outraged!

I invited Hubby to join in my sanctimony. "Oh," he said sheepishly, "they might have talked to me."

Dang it. It would do no good to rant and rail, to gnash my teeth and implore him to pass important messages like this—messages that concern our son's expulsion from school—to the family's administrative assistant—me. It would do no good, and I already knew the reason why. Things like this don't tend to make an impression on Hubby because they don't bounce back on him.

The next time he walks into that school, nobody is going to look the slightest bit disapprovingly at him. On the contrary, they will probably be delighted that he has shown up at all. I am not going to fare nearly as well.

Now, I'm "That Mom"—the one who just can't quite get it together. And, curses, this is a new school, a clean slate. For all anyone knows, I am an uber-mom who feeds her children only organically grown produce and passes the time on car trips playing Mensa brain-building games.

But not now. Now I'm an irresponsible slacker who can't even be bothered to immunize her children, never mind fulfilling a simple request from the school.

You think I am exaggerating? When my two eldest kids were little, I didn't work. It was easy for me to volunteer at their school. It was close to our house, it didn't require any clothing more formal than yoga pants, and all their little friends would run to the door to hug me when I arrived. Besides which, none of the little rug rats had surpassed my mathematical knowledge, so I still seemed like a genius.

I loved volunteering, and the staff loved me. Then we adopted our three youngest kids, the school was relocated far away from our house, and I opened a small business with one friend and zero employees. Things got complicated—and busy.

I didn't realize how far I had fallen from those heady days, until I said hello to one of the longtime staff members during one of my daughter's Student of the Month programs. (Clearly, she succeeds despite her slovenly mother.) "Oh, there you are," she cooed sweetly. "I was beginning to think the kids didn't have a mother."

Ouch.

Let me just say this: I have five kids. They have been attending public schools for thirteen years now. In all that time, we have not missed a single program our kids have participated in. Okay, that's a lie. One time—*one*—I fell asleep on the couch waiting to leave for an afternoon program. You would think that after seven years the statute of limitations would run out on that one. But, *noooo*.

All that hard work. All those years of cutting out paper rainbows for bulletin boards, of sorting flash cards into individual baggies, of wiping up spilled milk, poof. Gone. As if they never happened. Now it's all "What have you done for us lately?"

Hubby doesn't face this kind of rejection. Schools are so desperate for positive male role models that all he has to do is not abandon the kids at a gas station and the teachers love him. Show up at one parent/teacher conference and he might as well start clearing space on the mantle for his Father of the Year trophy.

He shouldn't be so comfortable with this. He should be outraged that the expectations are so low. He is, this latest snafu notwithstanding, a dedicated and involved father. He should demand more accountability for himself and other fathers. He should be the one taking the boy-child to the doctor, but he won't be. That would be me. I've already sweet-talked the scheduler at our clinic, and the boy will be back in school before the end of first period. Damn right, uber-Mom.

The whole thing cuts me so deeply because my only real aspiration in life, the only thing I've ever wanted to be, was someone who had her shit together, pardon my French.

Other kids wanted to be actors, dancers, teachers, astronauts. Not me. I just wanted to be the sort of person who drove a reliable car, had a purse free of receipts and used Kleenex, and always sent birthday cards on time. Instead, I was a chubby, unorganized kid who grew into a chubby and unorganized adult. I've got five kids, raccoons living under the roof of my house, a cat with chronic bladder control issues, and I wouldn't show you the inside of my purse on a bet.

In retrospect, I blame my grandparents.

My grandparents had their shit together, or so it seemed to me. Their house was calm and drama-free, smelled like coffee and bacon, and was where we went when life was boring, challenging, or chaotic.

I was there a lot.

My grandpa was a farmer, our family's reigning rummy champion, and remains the handsomest man I have ever seen. My grandma sang along with the radio, would serve us bowls of ice cream with saltine crackers, and had a great pair of legs. I loved the walk over the hill, across the cornfield to the farm. I loved their easy laughter, helping with barn chores, and especially the many dessert choices available every single night at my grandma's table.

My mom and dad couldn't help but suffer in the comparison. Our house was homework and sibling rivalry and, one unfortunate summer, helping butcher and then clean and pluck chickens for the freezer. This is just the sort of chore that leads to the desire to be somewhere, anywhere, else.

Oh, the joy of being one generation removed. More than anything, what my grandparents had going for them was not having to live with us, their adoring grandchildren. I know that now, having a brood of my own. It's easy to appear calm and serene, to laugh—ha-ha-ha—at the spilt milk or the broken plate, when you know the little darlings will be going home soon.

Also, and most importantly, grandparents are not responsible for the misdeeds of the youth. No one, upon seeing a child pitch a fit in the grocery store, thinks, "Wow, those grandparents really spoiled that one." Being a parent is just an overwhelming, decades-long, hot-house of stress. Oh, probably not for YOU. You are more than likely one of those sorts who adore parenthood and the miracle of new life, who wonder at the inner working of your child's brain as evidenced by the delightful bon mots that tumble from his or her lips like pearls.

Well, goody for you.

I was like you once, back when our firstborn, Miss Teen Wonder, was an only child. now, with two, three, four, five children, I find my view of parenting has changed considerably. Back then, Hubby and I were all, "Our child is a genius. We shall dedicate our lives to making sure she gets into Harvard, in order to pave the way for her Nobel Peace Prize."

Now, our stated goal is:"Four out of five *not* incarcerated."

I'm not even kidding.

Increasing our brood from one to five has definitely altered both our expectations and our parenting styles. Once, I had a solid chance of pulling it together. I was home so I had a lot more time. The volume in our house was definitely lower, it was reasonably clean, and I still had the energy and optimism to plan for the future.

Now our home is in free fall. It's like a never-ending ultimate fighting cage match in our house, where all the combatants are battling for the last cookie and who gets control of the television. (Answer: Mom and Mom, if you know what's good for you.) I don't so much plan for the future as I have a countdown clock to the date our youngest graduates high school. Hubby occasionally hugs the little ones and tells them that they can live at home as long as they want, a move that invariably earns him a dirty look from me. I am sorry. I love those kids, but NO.

I will never get my shit together if these children do not leave my house. I have somewhat, though barely, accepted the premise that I am going to be disheveled, late, and chunky while they are here, but I refuse to embrace the concept that it might be my natural and permanent state. I choose to believe in a golden future time when my home will be tidy, my bank account will be flush, and my furniture will be white. None of that will happen if the little darlings live with us forever, no matter what hubby wants. The disorder and chaos don't seem to affect him as much, but then again, he isn't the cruise director on this little boat of ours.

Of course, being the eternal optimist that I am, I never stop believing that there is some technique, practice, new organizational system, or mantra that will immediately transform me into a flawless, impeccable human being. Currently, this is playing out in my recent decision to not start a single task, unless I have the time and energy to complete it in that moment.

My house hasn't been cleaned in a month.

I'm a lover of efficient systems, and it occurred to me that I am operating in a very inefficient one. I am forever starting one of those interminable tasks that fill my day, realizing I am missing some crucial component, usually the desire to do the stupid thing in the first place, and end up abandoning it for some vague, future date. As a result, I end up making two or three false starts before the task becomes too overwhelming to ignore.

This is not efficient.

Take my email: I think I currently have five hundred unread emails between my various mailboxes. Normally, I check email, like most people, several times a day, scrolling quickly through the ever-growing list but never really taking any sort of action. The daily newsletter from some recipe site? Well, I have supper planned, but I might need some ideas another time, better leave it for another day. Ditto the newsletter of upcoming 5K races in my area: I don't have any desire to run one today, but you never know. I might be seized by the desire at any moment, and this list would be so handy. Never mind that experience has taught me the events will all be finished long before I ever even read the email. And that email from my son's middle school? Lord, I don't even want to know what that's about.

So they fester, the list of required actions growing ever longer, my dread deepening, and all the while I waste precious moments, checking and rechecking without actually accomplishing anything. If I merely procrastinate the entire task until I am mentally prepared to take action, the job becomes much more efficient. Sure, there are still five hundred emails waiting for me, but five hundred emails I only have to look at once. Let's call that a win.

Additionally, I have this bad habit, of taking on big projects or challenges, getting overwhelmed, praying mightily that they will end, and then, once the pressure subsides a bit? BAM! New project. Why am I telling you this? Because I am going to reform, I swear.

(Okay, so I've already signed up for next year's marathon, but right after that I'm going to relax.)

There is just something in my DNA, deep within my stalwart, German farm-girl upbringing that clings to be belief that "If it doesn't hurt, it doesn't count."

While, admittedly, a useful mantra when pushing through any of life's difficulties, I'm starting to see where holding this thought might incline one to make things more difficult than they technically need to be.

A friend of mine, wiser and far more mentally well-balanced than I tend to be, has taken to asking me, "What if it all was easy?"

The first time she asked, I just looked at her as if she were crazy. Easy? Have you seen my life? Have I never told you of our schedules, the demands, and how the children are systematically destroying our home, one permanent marker stain at a time?

Easy? Phfft. The woman must be nuts.

Then she asked me again. And again. And it started to occur to me, well, what if? What if she is right and all this struggling is merely me, trying to make my life significant in some masochistic, unholy way? The kids don't seem to be struggling, and they are living in the same, cluttered home that I am. Hubby? Well, he just glides on through. The only thing that bothers him is the rising stress level of his crazy wife.

Oh, crap. It isn't the kids. It's me.

The Sunshine Rules

I often think we have stages of life that we are more suited to than others, a time of life that really hits our particular skill set and rarely brings our fears and insecurities bubbling to the surface. For example, I was excellent during college. I mean, I was *great*. I was happy all the time. I had moved from a small Wisconsin town where I felt uncomfortable, ill-suited, and anxious to a large city where I had mindblowing freedom. Nobody cared how I dressed or what I believed or who I was because everybody was dressing, believing, and being exactly who they felt themselves to be. It was glorious.

No one cared what music I listened to, if I went to class, what my grades were, where I lived, or how many tattoos I got. Worry was for other people. Specifically, as I look back on it now, for my parents. They had to have been beside themselves wondering what the hell their little girl was doing with her life. Where I saw freedom of expression, independence, and joy, they no doubt saw financial irresponsibility and a life dedicated to the lowest rungs of the food service industry.

Likewise, I was great when my kids were babies. I have never before nor since been such a paragon of patience. I was breathlessly infatuated with every little morsel of their bodies. When the babies cried, I became, not a shrieking harpy of stress, as my current state might suggest, but the cooing-est, kissy-est, gentlest mom in all the land. Well, maybe 80 percent of the time. Twenty percent of the time I might have cried along with them, but that was in solidarity and not born of resentment and bitterness, I swear. My point is: I was good at being a mother, at one time.

But this stage—this stage of mortgages and jobs and half-grown, sassy children? It's torture. I am not good at this. I do not skate through my days with joy in my heart, simply from the great fortune of being alive. Oh, hell no. I worry incessantly; I fret all the time. Disaster looms large in my imagination, stalking the kids, their future, our property and livelihoods, our family members. I am exhausted by the need to stay vigilant because my own superstitious nature believes whatever is coming won't be nearly as bad if I can catch it early. Which is ridiculous. If something truly catastrophic ever happens, you just know it's going to sneak up on me from behind, while I stare, wild-eyed into the empty horizon. Don't blame me; that's just how it works, I think.

Happiness. Why is it so hard for so many of us? When it gets down to it, I think it is a simple equation: happiness = contentment + commitment to the present moment. It doesn't seem as if it should be so difficult, but it is. Luckily I have role models. One thing that Hubby shares with my father is the ability to exist in the here and now. I'm not sure how they do it. Both are maddeningly immune to the lure of "what if?" (Doom! Disaster!) I'll be rambling on about some potential trouble, and Hubby will smile at me and in a reassuring voice assure me that we are fine.

Well, sure, *right now* we are, which is not my point at all. Too bad for me, though, because Hubby refuses to join in the crazy-making and remains stalwartly serene. It's more than a little annoying.

Neither am I doing well on the contentment front. We are fortunate to live in an area of the world where you would think this shouldn't be a problem. Everyone is healthy and has access to clean water and ibuprofen. We have three couches on which to lounge at the end of a day of productive work, and my home is flush with luxurious foodstuffs—avocados and cashews and wasabi peas abound. Truly, the greatest problems currently in my life are trying to find a Sunday afternoon yoga class and the fact that I have to wait too long between seasons of *Downton Abbey*.

I think I'll live.

Still, that carefree happiness of the past seems nearly impossible to achieve now, despite my frequent attempts to just calm down and relax, dang nabbit. Or at least, it did. Seems I've been overlooking a secret weapon. It's come to my attention, embarrassingly late in the game, that I am living with a real-life spiritual master. Forget running off to India to study, legs growing numb in lotus, at the feet of a maddeningly serene yogi. No need to attend a silent retreat run by a wise and beatific elderly nun. Here, in my home, I have discovered a soul who seems to have unlocked the secrets to eternal happiness, and oddly enough, this soul resides in the body of a thirteen-year-old girl.

It must be the inner turmoil brought on by the past few years that finally opened my eyes to what was right in front of me. Closing my business, ushering Miss Teen Wonder off to college, losing my much loved grandmother, the looming realization that—to paraphrase Meg Ryan—I'm going to be fifty . . . *someday*, all these have left me, wandering in an internal funk, constantly asking the question, "What the hell am I doing with my life anyway?" And there, dancing, most often literally, around the periphery was my daughter. Let's call her "Sunshine."

Sunshine is half of the amazing duo—the twin girls—in the middle of our family. She is tiny but sturdy, with a laugh that seems far too big for the bitty body she inhabits. She has a thousand-watt smile and hair as big as her heart. She is up for anything, always. When I grow up, I want to be just like her.

I'm not sure how she has managed to amass such an affinity for happiness and contentment at such a young age. She is, as I mentioned, a twin. Perhaps rather than splitting the DNA down the middle, each girl received total possession of a few gifts. Her sister is fiercely competitive (a trait Sunshine has not a trace of) and unwaveringly confident. She sees big-time success in her future, and if you knew her, you'd believe it, too. However, she lacks Sunshine's easy equanimity or Sunshine's ability to flow through life unencumbered with tedious minutia. Take, for example, the practical application of volume. When trying to store a sizable amount of leftover soup in the refrigerator, many of us might choose to use, say, a large container, rather than roughly twenty-seven half-pint mason jars. Not my kids, however. When I open the refrigerator doors and spy a sea of tiny glass bottles, all containing the same, exact substance, I feel as if my brain might explode. It doesn't bother Sunshine one whit. She'll cheerfully rummage through the lot, looking for the mustard or the last bit of salami, happy as a clam. I don't think she has an idea that there is any other way to be in the world. And that is my new directive as her mother—to make sure that she never does.

My other goal is to study her like a lab rat to learn what she so effortlessly knows. Here is what I've sussed out so far:

The Sunshine Rules

1. Happiness isn't (or shouldn't be) dependent on your circumstances. The fact that you are awake and breathing is reason enough to break into song. Sunshine wakes up happy. Is she headed to school? To run errands with her dad? Spending the day cleaning her room? It's all good. Happiness for me is much more conditional. The answers to the questions "What do I have to do today?" "Do these jeans still fit?" or "Are we out of coffee?" affect me far more than they should.

2. Music is magic. Sunshine is never *not* singing, hence she moves through the house, not with the determined head-down, goose-stepping march of her mother (I've got things to DO, people!) but with a perpetual shimmy. If you are accompanied by your own soundtrack, every waking moment is a dance party. Plenty of spiritual traditions give credence to the uplifting power of certain audio vibrations—I just didn't imagine that the Demi Lovato songbook was, in fact, a hymnal of sorts.

3. Be a cheerleader. Now this is something Sunshine and her sister share. They are unflaggingly, unceasingly, unerringly supportive. They are never—not ever—jealous. If something good happens to the folks around them, they are as happy as if it were happening to them. Check out Sunshine's Facebook page. If you post any good news, any at all, "My baby just turned one!" or "Loved this movie!" or "Delicious lunch with friends." Sunshine will not just "like" your post; she will sprinkle it with emojis, the likes of which you have never before seen. Who doesn't feel on top of the world when she responds to your new profile pic with, "You are GOR-GEOUS!!!!!! (kissy face, kissy face, heart, heart, winking cat, heart, high five, cat high five, thumbs up)?" It is my favorite thing in the world, and one I have already started using my-self. The fact that you do not have such enthusiastic cheer-leaders in your life, well, I just feel plain sorry for you.

I don't know if any of this is helpful to you, but I feel as if my own life gets dramatically better when I remember to follow The Sunshine Rules. I've read literally hundreds of books dedicated to unlocking the secret of a happy and contented life, and none of them have been as effective as Sunshine's effortless wisdom: Be happy where you are, sing a little song, and encourage the people around you. Enlighten-ment in three easy steps. Oh, sure, there are other lessons I could add to the list such as "It never hurts to look fabulous" or "Glitter nail polish is the best antidepressant," but if I stick to the big three, I think I'll be all right.

Older and Not a Bit Wiser

My stupid husband gave me a hickey the other day.

That's right, just laugh it up. I'm walking around in turtle-necks, like the world's first geriatric teenager, because Mr. Romance got all bitey on me. God only knows how long this is going to last, since my skin doesn't bounce back like it used to. If I pinch at my face, I instantly bruise, and God forbid I sleep on my side, my face pressed to the pillow; I spend the entire morning looking like a Shar-Pei puppy.

Puppy, I wish. Some days I *feel* eighty and *look* like I'm a hundred and twelve. And I'm not the only one noting our advancing years. Recently, Hubby and I had the following conversation:

Hubby: We're getting old.

Me: I know.

Hubby: No, *old.*

Me: I KNOW!

Hubby: OLD!

Riveting stuff. Maybe not as gripping as "Who left the lights on?" but definitely more engaging than "Where are my reading glasses?"

He was acting as if, somehow, I didn't understand the gravity of the situation. Let me tell you, the other day I rested my upper arm in an open car window and it was as if I had unfurled a parade flag. Trust me, I understand gravity.

I understand a lot of other things, too, that are directly related to my advancing age, such as the appeal of comfortable shoes and the dangers of Icy Hot abuse. When I was younger, I had no idea that one could throw out one's back simply by sneezing. Now I do. Additionally, I simply lacked the knowledge that the human body was capable of growing a single follicle of slender, black hair two inches in length over the course of *one night* and having it appear in the morning, a nocturnal gift sprouting from one's shoulder or cheek.

Not that I'm against getting older. Quite the contrary. I see the cringe-worthy lengths to which some people go to "maintain" their youth and draw back in horror. I don't know when we decided that shooting plastic and botulism into our faces was better than a simple softening of the skin. I think, after a certain point, it must be the incongruity between the person we internally feel ourselves to be and the reflection we see in the mirror. As for me, I have felt pretty much the same since I was sixteen years old, maybe even younger. Not that I haven't grown or changed but there is a sameness as to how I interact with the world.

If I were walking around in the dark and bumped into myself, I would recognize me, no matter what my age. There's a continuity to my inner self that has nothing to do with this graying, saggy-chested, chin-hair sprouting woman I find looking back at me most mornings in the mirror. I spend an inordinate amount of time peering at the mirror, cocking my head from side to side, like an inquisitive sparrow, wondering, "Is that what I look like now?"

And the changes just keep coming. I recently went through an enormous battle, attempting to wrestle my hair back to its natural color after a cool quarter of a century of dyeing it red. In my opinion, the only thing saving this mousey brown mess is the two pronounced streaks of gray running from my temples. I really love them, in fact. I think they make me look like a super-villain—if only I had a cape and a plan to take over Gotham. I call them my Temples of Doom. My son couldn't disagree more. "You have got to dye your hair, Mom," he implores. "When men go gray, they look distinguished. Women just look old."

This is from the image conscious one of the family, the one kid who's making a deliberate bid to be cool. Whereas the other kids happily introduce me to their friends and teachers, my son would rather hide me under a plain brown bag. It's as if the sight of my gray hair has brought on a temporary bout of amnesia in my son and he has forgotten that I am the boss of this house and, through the awesome feat of possessing a valid driver's license, his social life. So, good luck with that, kid.

Though at the time I didn't know it, growing up as somewhat of a geek has definitely helped me down the line. What image do I have to cling to? My physical self has never been so heaped with accolades that I'm terrified to let it go. On the contrary, who the hell cares? I have always been invested in being quirky, funny, and smart—though admittedly I worked less on that last one than the others. (What? Smart is hard.) Gray hair doesn't change that plan. In fact, the strategy for my future style, which is decidedly not cool dependent, involves chunky silver jewelry, red lipstick, and low-top sneakers. Geez, my son probably won't even let me in his house.

Wouldn't matter if he did. Depending on how many steps he has on his front porch, I might just elect to stay in the car. I am so very tired, so very much of the time. It's probably some sort of biological defense mechanism. It is harder to get worked up over, say, my graying errant facial hair when I have such a limited amount of energy. At my age, I have to pick my battles, and I simply cannot waste my finite energy supply on vanity. I'm far too busy trying to convince my husband that our lack of a dishwasher constitutes elder abuse.

Aging provides plenty of such self-defense mechanisms. Maybe our diminishing eyesight is meant to protect us from having a stroke every time we look in the mirror. It is absolutely no mistake that our near vision starts to go at the exact same time as our chins begin to sag like a sock full of marbles. It is a biological kindness, and it keeps your partner looking that much more attractive, too.

You know what? I'm glad to see my vision go. Glad, I say. Back when I didn't need reading glasses to floss my teeth, I would spend a certain amount of time every day nose to nose with my reflection in the mirror. I ask you, when you are peering that intently at your reflection, have you ever been looking for something good? Are you leaning in and thinking, "I am just so adorable; let me get in here really close and appreciate the twinkle in my eyes"? Nope. Hell no. You, just like me, are looking for wrinkles, imperfections, and more recently, moles whose shifting boundaries might necessitate a trip to the dermatologist. I'm glad it's more difficult to see all that stuff now. It makes it easier to be a friend to myself. Just this morning, I said to my reflection, "Wow, I look ten years younger than I am. How do I do it?" It was a conscious and bald-faced lie but the kind of thing you would tell a friend. (Except my friends. You all really do look ridiculously young, honest.) See that right there? That's called growth.

Some days when I think I am growing as a person, I have the occasional relapse, and it is rarely pretty. Take the time when Hubby decided to inform me that I'd been a bit "intense" as of late. He then went on to hypothesize that my declining hormone levels might be the culprit.

I stared at him blandly for a long moment, mentally contemplating which method of murdering him I would be most likely to get away with before stalking, silently from the room.

Understand that there was a time when that singular comment from Hubby would have led to a long night of nowhere good for him. I am excellent in an argument. I am tenacious, and six years of junior and senior high school speech competitions have developed my ability to dissect opposing opinions with the precision and enthusiasm of Dr. Frankenstein in his lab. I try not to use my gift for evil, but there have been times when it proved irresistible.

But not this night. I have a theory that most our fights are caused not by any real transgression but because one or both parties need a damn nap. Now, I try to ask myself before engaging in any sort of conflict, "Am I going to care about this in the morning?" So, I pondered the question: Was this discussion with Hubby big enough to invest my waking hours in? The answer was a resounding *no*. I crawled into bed and spent an enjoyable couple of hours reading. I was feeling rather proud of myself for being so darn mature, when Hubby burst into our room *furious*.

He accused me of giving him the silent treatment and didn't believe my protests that I was merely "taking a little space." I told him I wasn't mad at all, honest.

Except I clearly was.

So there is the kind of maturity when you hear your husband's criticisms and do not actually dismiss them off the cuff. Then there is the actual maturity that happens when you can state *out loud*—not just silently to yourself—that there is the slightest chance that he might be right, but you would prefer to ponder that alone, please. Obviously, I hadn't evolved quite that much.

I leapt out of bed, enacted a deep bow, and said, "Thank you, honey, for your profound insights as to my many character flaws. I cannot tell you how happy you have made me by drawing attention to my miserable behavior. Thank you, thank you, thank you."

He laughed. Honestly, I wasn't quite sure I meant it as light-heartedly as he took it, but immediately our moods improved. I only admit the entire episode to you in order to remind myself that "old" isn't necessarily the same as "mature."

In fact, it behooves me to get better at owning up to all the stupid things I do because I swear that the older I get, the more frequently they occur. I was in the SuperTarget parking lot the other day (actually there is a good chance that I am in the SuperTarget parking lot on any given day; I might be there right now), and I was having problems with the strap of my shirt. I couldn't quite reach far enough behind me to adjust it, and, without really considering the wisdom of my actions, I whipped my shirt off, fixed the offending strap, and wiggled back into my top.

I had somehow forgotten that I was in a public parking lot, and the windshield of my car was constructed, as most windshields are, of transparent glass. When I exited the car, I noticed the gentleman returning from the cart corral was aggressively avoiding eye contact.

Without the slightest effort on his part, he had already gotten to second base. I tried not to be insulted that he didn't seem to have enjoyed it.

I feel that this is not a mistake I would have made when I was younger. In our youth, we are obsessed with how people perceive us: Do we seem smart? Funny? Cute? Is our ignorance as painfully obvious as we suspect it is? In my teen years, I often felt as if I were under the same intense scrutiny as an actor in the spotlight. And that giddy energy we all had? I believe now it was nothing more than stage fright. The fact that I have become so oblivious as to appear semi-nude in a busy parking lot is pretty much a triumph of age over the concerns of ego—at least, that's what I'm telling myself.

Which brings me to denial.

As I was peering into the mirror this week—again, nothing good comes from this—I became engrossed with the state of my skin. Forget the wrinkles; forget the crow's feet; forget, if you can, the fledgling turkey waddle. My skin, itself, has taken on a certain loose, feathery texture, one I remember loving in my grandmothers. I was seriously infatuated with their fuzzy, soft faces and took them to be, like the always present smells of baby powder, coffee, and pork, just a physical manifestation of the loving, gentle spirits they were.

Needless to say, I do not find my own loose, feathery skin lovely. I find it alarming. I find it disturbing to the point of provoking a mental breakdown. While my grandmothers' skin was clearly an endearing and undeniable sign of advanced age, I have decided that my skin is simply dry, proving once again the protective power of denial and the human mind. Clearly, the problem is my hippie dippy moisturizer. Since I have started working in an eco-store, I have learned more than you would want to know about the ingredients in face creams. Use a commercial face lotion? Might as well just rub WD-40 onto your skin. So I switched to an all-natural, no known carcinogens, no petroleum-based chemical ingredient moisturizer. The result: my skin looks like an unraveling roll of crepe paper. Who knew petroleum was an anti-aging ingredient?

Some of you might point out that switching moisturizers really had nothing to do with the state of my skin. That I cannot expect my forty-six-year-old skin to look like my twenty-year-old skin did. You might maintain that maturity has its own, innate beauty and that I should embrace the wisdom and loveliness of this age. To you, I say, "What have I ever done to you?"

I try hard to rise above the current cultural obsession with all things "anti-aging." As a feminist and as a sporadic spiritual seeker, I find it crass and overtly misogynistic and decidedly not "higher mind." I had thought that I was succeeding in this effort, when, in reality, the shit had not yet hit the fan. It is easy to mentally embrace aging when you are still relatively young, when the occasional creak is more hilarious than chronic, when you are med-free and still cute enough to occasionally warrant a wink and a smile from a flirty stranger. I still receive that type of attention, by the way, it's just that, for the past several years, the flirting has all been from elderly retirees.

I try not to think about it too much.

This recent debacle with my skin has forced me to throw any sort of equanimity I thought I'd achieved right out the window. You know you are not spiritually evolved when you hold two jars of face cream in your hand, weigh cancer risks against wrinkles, and decide what you want is to look really, really good at your chemo appointments.

It would be much easier to take if my skin was the only thing sagging. See, this is why I don't trust the Universe at all. I said, "Dear Lord, allow me to embrace aging with grace," and whatever power exists said, "Okee doke" and suddenly I looked like a shrunken, over-ripe banana. I suppose this is because you can't really embrace a thing unless you have it. It's my fault really. I should have been more specific. What I should have said was, "Dear Lord, allow me to embrace the aging of others with grace, while I remain as dewy and untouched as a mountain flower by a stream."

So now it's all coming undone. Things are changing faster than I can come to terms with them. This is not how I want to approach getting older. I want to be calm and serene, confident and energetic.

I want to be more concerned with the quality of my soul than the appearance of my skin. But it is *hard*.

Of course, the wrinkles aren't truly the problem, are they? The profound changes in our appearances, the ones that render us unrecognizable to ourselves, are really just a concrete reminder of all things that have passed. Day to day, we scurry along, conscious that time is ticking. But it isn't often we let ourselves feel that sense of loss. Some days, you can tell me that it's been twenty-eight years since I graduated high school and I'll simply shrug, indifferently. You can show me pictures of the grandchildren of the kids I used to babysit and I might manage a half-hearted, "Wow." But sometimes, when I am in a particular mood and bumping around alone in my house for longer than would be prudent, the thought surfaces that once I was six years old and my grandpa would let me sit on his lap and steer the tractor and that moment will never, *ever* happen again. Puddles. Buckets of tears. I look in the mirror and think, "I don't *want* to be the grandma. I want to be the grandkid, the teen watching Monty Python at her best friend's house, the young mom with a new baby. How can that all be gone?" Silly, I know. But, *damn*.

Once a week, I spend time at a home for older women with various kinds of memory loss. As you can imagine, you become close to the residents. There is one woman who has taken to telling me stories of her and her husband. I'm always drawn in because it reminds me so much of my husband and me. But every story ends with the phrase, "And you know, it's been seven years since he passed and I think about him every day. I miss him so much," and then tears. Which makes me think I should just pack up and leave Hubby right now. Frankly, I'm feeling kind of fragile, and I don't really need the aggravation.

But it wouldn't really stop the loss, would it? The best we can do is recognize that each moment zips by heartbreakingly fast and embrace the new experiences ahead. Maybe someday, God willing, I'll be the grandma; we already know I have the skin for it. And maybe, if I am so lucky, I will be given the chance to share all my best memories—to sing the same songs, play the same games, bake the same cookies—bringing me closer, at least in my heart, to the times and people I've loved so much.

I just need to find a tractor.

Grace Under Pressure—Someday

I might have mentioned that one of the benefits of aging is the ability to accept minor humiliations more graciously. Because, really, what choice do I have? Every day my body displays some new, ridiculous, and, more often than not, disgusting trait that I can do absolutely nothing about. Right now, we are in the dead of winter, end of February in Minnesota—a time that tests your very soul. I haven't been outside willingly in weeks; I'm suffering winter-induced depression; I'm at my yearly chunkiest, so nothing fits; I can't sleep; running has fallen by the wayside; and yesterday, I had to shave my neck. I almost ended it all by heading outside to lay face-first in the yard: death by snowbank.

It takes a leap to make peace with the fact that you now have to regularly shave your damn chin. Most my girlfriends won't do it; they're still tweezing away, which means I am either smarter or hairier than they are. It's probably hairier.

I came out to my best girlfriend as an unusually hairy middle-age lady one evening when some pretty crappy circumstances demanded that we drink many bottles of wine. This engendered in me such a feeling of solidarity that I offered up the most intimate shame I had at the time, and I let her feel my bristly chin. Understand that I knew this was a silly little gesture, but woman-to-woman, it *is* unsettling. Her shocked, heartfelt laughter somehow made me feel better, as if she'd hugged me and said, "Right, this is some *messed up shit.*"

So yesterday, I'm sitting at a red light, and I flip down the mirror visor to check my lipstick only to discover, dear God, that I am growing a neck beard. A snowy, fluffy neck beard. And they wonder why women lose interest in sex. It's hard to get all motivated when you know that no matter what you do, you are going to look like chubby Senior Muttonchops in lingerie—and nobody wants to see that. Word.

I stormed home, backed my husband into a corner, and pointed my finger like a lance demanding that he add to my living will (Working title: "Hell no! I won't go!") that my home health care nurse be proficient with a razor. The way I figure it, if my grandfather could manage to present a cleanly shaven face to the world every day of his life, by God, so can I. The last thing I want is to awaken from some medically induced trauma, look in the mirror, and see the white, flowing beard of Rip Van Winkle. It could happen. They way I sprout chin hairs, it could happen in as little as a week.

So this is clearly not one of the small humiliations I am accepting graciously. However, there are many other errors and foibles I enact that no longer seem to bother me as much. "At least it isn't a neck beard," I tell myself when confronted with yet another mistake I've made, and whistling a merry tune, I continue with my day. Hit with a late fee for forgetting to mail the credit card bill? "At least it isn't a neck beard." Dropped the ball at work? "Could be worse, could be a neck beard."

Hubby absolutely hates when I joke about this. He also hates when I tell people that my new theme song is "Macho Man" by the Village People. He thinks I'm being too mean to myself. But, to my way of thinking, it isn't me that is being mean. My traitorous body has turned on me, and I am just along, unwillingly, for the ride.

Not all the experts agree with me on this. Recently, while ambling through the chapters of a new, self-helpy sort of book, I came upon the admonishment to "Ditch the self-deprecating humor" on the basis that it is basically a plea to the world to not take you seriously. Um, *what*, now? I can't do that! Making fun of myself is how I get through the day, how I manage to keep a throttle hold on the perfectionist side of myself and maintain whatever sliver of good humor I have about things like neck beards. If I can't poke fun at me, I am definitely turning on the rest of the world, and no one is going to like that.

Still, that bit of advice stuck with me and I asked a co-worker what she thought. Is revealing and mocking my falling estrogen levels (and subsequent Grizzly Adams facial hair) funny or pathetic?

"Oh, good Lord," she said, "we *have* to laugh at it. It's horrifying."

That's the word: "horrifying." All laughter aside, this whole premenopausal carnival is a train wreck. My waist is disappearing. My boobs are deflating, and I am increasingly becoming monochromatic—whatever dewy pinkness that used to live in my lips and cheeks is long gone. I am losing my femininity by the second. Laughing at the whole ridiculous mess is just about the healthiest thing I could be doing. Hubby is worried, though. He thinks this adds up to a whole bunch of self-loathing, which despite my assurances to the contrary, has him all worked up. Bless his heart.

I could mention to him, that if anyone is being less than sympathetic to the poor, middle-aged women out there, he might want to take a gander at his own rotten gender. I recently read an article, the contents of which I immediately relegated to the "Duh" file, that reported on researchers studying the online dating habits of people over forty. They figured out that while both men and women wanted to remain attractive to the opposite sex, only women were interested in partners of their own age. Yes, someone spent time and money to come up with a conclusion that men like younger women. Like I said, *duh*.

Maybe I should feel sorry for men. Maybe the problem lies, hypothetically, with men's vulnerability while facing their declining virility. To feel current and virile, they need to see that they can excite a youthful partner. Certainly, facing their diminishing influence is a serious issue that we women should be sensitive to. Lord. I barely kept a straight face while writing that. What I want to say is, "Boo freaking hoo." Which demonstrates one of the reasons why men over forty wouldn't want to date me.

Lack of sympathy aside, dating someone younger just doesn't make sense to me. But that's because I am one of those saps who likes my partner to be a peer. I cannot wrap my brain around the current "cougar" phenomenon because I see males in their twenties as infants, babes in the woods, not potential sexual partners. Ick. I like a man, baby. With thick forearms, a little paunch, and a receding hairline. Oh, yeah, *sexy*. I don't want someone whose main concern is finding his next gig waiting tables. I giggle at the earnest quest of discovery that such men are on. I want someone who understands the gravity of losing a job when you have a family and a mortgage, not someone worried about paying the rent on his efficiency apartment and feeding his iguana. I want someone who has suffered loss and disappointment, so that he can fully appreciate the bittersweet, fragile nature of life, not someone who still thinks he's invulnerable.

Life is short and sweet and terrible and wondrous all at the same time, and due to no fault of their own, the youth cannot appreciate it fully. Of course, those are the very reasons that send men streaming to my younger counterparts. They want to bathe themselves in that invulnerable attitude, to feel strong and brave like they did when they were younger, to forget that bitter sweetness of life, for a while. So they look for someone young and not afraid.

Friends of mine who are out in that dating pool say how common it is for men to be turned off by women who are self-sufficient. They say men don't like women who can take care of themselves. I can't for a minute understand this. According to my sources, they want a woman who is helpless, who can't change a tire or replace an electrical switch. Really? Have you ever tried to get a man to do anything? Good Lord. Just try to get the bathroom cleaned or a faucet replaced. It's like a slow, non-medicated tooth extraction. I would think men would want women who know how to do *everything* because it's that much less likely they will be asked to perform manual labor. See how much I know? It's a good thing I'm married; I'd have no idea how to maneuver this crazy environment. Plus, being a woman over forty, I have zero patience and I *will* tell you if I think something is BS. And Lord help you if it is. Besides, should something ever happen to Hubby, God forbid, I haven't decided if I will even date again, period.

Now don't get me wrong. I love being married. I love my husband, and he is a great companion and source of support. However. Have you ever noticed how rare it is that widowers remain unmarried, whereas plenty of widows say, "Meh. Not so much, thank you"? It's not an indictment of their marriages or spouses. It has to do with freedom.

So much of a woman's life is tied up in caring for other people. It's our default. Kids really bring it home, of course, but I know plenty of women without children who spend inordinate amounts of time smoothing the way for partners or friends. I'm convinced we have a whole lobe of the brain dedicated to concerns about others such as if our friends need us to water their plants during their vacation and whether that twenty-something at the bar (whom we don't even know) should've brought a warm sweater.

So when we find ourselves alone at the end of life, we wonder: why the hell would we jump right back into taking care of someone else? Like I said, meh, no thanks. Does that sound mean? I don't intend for it to, except on those days when I'm pissed and overworked and then I do.

I want my kids to feel cared for. I want to be a help and support to Hubby. I believe that what I do adds value to our lives right up until the point that it all becomes a freaking, huge, overwhelming imposition. Then I hate everybody. My switch is flipped to evil, and the next person who asks me "Where is the peanut butter?" is getting a firestorm of resentment rained down upon them. Scorched earth, baby. Even I know that it isn't fair when that comes out of nowhere, and yet, it is impossible to predict or prevent. Maybe if the little buggers weren't quite so complacent about it. Maybe if it wasn't a given that Mom would knock herself out for everyone. It could be that it isn't my problem at all and that some people are simply spoiled little ingrates. Perhaps, if people didn't act like English lords speaking to a serf, we might not have an issue.

See how fast that switch flips? It seems to be the ingratitude that really sets me off. I perform Herculean feats of productivity every day and it's all, "Pfft. Of course." Maybe that's why I started running marathons. Sure, it's 26.2 painful miles, but it's 26.2 painful miles of people applauding your efforts. Seems worth it to me, 'cause ain't nobody applauding around my house. To be fair (so unlike me), the kids and Hubby aren't the only ones who are susceptible to this. I could, if pressed, admit that I can take folks, and by that I mean Hubby, for granted as well. It may even tie back to men preferring younger women.

Let's be honest, younger men are largely clueless. Outside of beer pong and whatever the newest version of *Call of Duty* is, they have no idea what they are doing. Older men have been in relationships long enough that they have learned, or had it beaten into them, that there are certain things women expect. I imagine that plenty of young women are dazzled by a guy who knows darn well that he better make a fuss over her birthday, that there had better be cake, goddamnit, and she doesn't want to be the person to bake it.

Oh, I'm sorry. Was this supposed to be the bit when I talk about how gracefully I am accepting life's little annoyances these days? I swear, just when I think I have maybe achieved some small level of Zen-like wisdom, I open my mouth and out flies the same peevish voice I have tried so hard to grow past. Which is a shame. Because if there were ever a body type I could realistically aspire to, a chubby, laughing Buddha is definitely within my grasp. Although, now that I think about it, all the Buddhas I have ever seen have a decided lack of facial hair. Nary a chin beard in sight. Sigh.

The Man of the House

What to say about my husband? Well, he's clearly the tolerant sort. But then again, so am I. Though we live in Minnesota, Land of Perpetual Snowfall, and it is currently the dead of winter, this man whom I have pledged to remain with through all the days of my life insists on running an industrial warehouse fan in our minuscule bedroom—because he likes the noise. Up until yesterday, I was extremely tolerant of this—that was when I discovered he is wearing earplugs to bed, the very earplugs I bought in self-defense to drown out the jet hangar like hum of the fan and his relentless snoring. Never has "Until death do us part" seemed like such an attractive option.

I understand that I am hardly the perfect spouse. I'm sure there are many things he wishes I would do differently, but I do not feel the least bit guilty. I simply do not have the energy for any sort of marital self-improvement because I am using it all to stifle the urge to smother him in his sleep.

That, my friends, is commitment.

I once knew a woman who put it thusly, "Some days I just love my husband so much, and other times I can't imagine spending the next ten minutes with him, never mind the rest of my life. Luckily, the feeling almost always passes."

You think I'm joking, but I'm not. I believe many, if not most, marriages that fail do so because partners get worn down by the mundane details of their everyday lives. They get ambushed by the normalcy of it all. We think love must remain a torrent of desire. What a crock. I am never more amused than when a relatively newly married friend confesses in hushed tones that they are not "in love" anymore.

"Finally," I think between chuckles, "it's about time."

This is, after all, the person you see every blessed day of your life, 365 days a year, year in, year out. Every. Single. Day.

I don't care if you're living with the Dalai Lama, after two weeks, he's going to get on your nerves.

But let's not forget ourselves here, women cannot, after all, maintain the "fragile flower" persona for long. A couple of near homicidal, hormonally induced fights and that myth is pretty well shot. I, myself, have wore my husband down with the standard, "Do I look fat?" line so often, I'm starting to annoy myself.

After you have a baby, it only gets worse. It becomes glaringly apparent that you and your husband really know very little about each other. Oh, sure, you are aware of each other's quirks and foibles; maybe even share the same politics or—more miraculously—the same taste in movies, but the moment that blessed little bundle of joy appears, all you thought you knew vanishes. Something as simple as whether or not to pick up the baby when it cries, which it does continuously, becomes an ongoing conflict of epic proportions. Not unlike fighting in the Middle East or a Michael Bay movie, it goes on and on.

Sometimes the conflict starts before the baby is even born. With my second pregnancy, my husband and I fought bitterly for nine straight months over whether or not to circumcise the baby, should it be a boy. (It was.) His logic went something like this: because I picked the name of our first-born daughter, he got to decide whether or not to lop off a perfectly good part of my little angel. I guess it's no secret which side I came down on. I have no doubt in my mind that, had he insisted on going through with it, I would have stood full upright in the stirrups, kicked aside any RNs in my path, grabbed the child, and hightailed it out of there, bare-assed to the world.

Luckily, I was not forced to resort to full-blown, mama bear insanity. My dear husband was with me throughout all the stages of labor, despite his extreme distaste of all things medical. He cannot stand the sight of blood or abide the utterance of such phrases as "soft tissue damage" or "exploratory procedure." Such squeamishness is an unexpected and surprisingly endearing trait in a man nearly six and a half feet tall, and the children and I have spent the past several decades tormenting him for our own amusement. Given that witnessing one of the kids rip off a Band-Aid to proudly display a particularly deep and gnarly scar causes him to hide his head in his sweatshirt, the violent expulsion of an actual child from my body rendered him helpless. He knew that the cost of expanding our family had come due and that I, not he, was the one left to pick up that particular check.

Acquiescing to my wishes in that moment was a wise move. It went a long way toward easing any lingering resentments or future recriminations.

But not all the way.

Life in those first few days after the birth of our child was beautiful. It really was. I felt such closeness with my husband and our new little family. And though the profound peace I enjoyed could have been due to the lingering drugs in my system, I felt a deep affection for the man with whom I had created this wondrous new life. But that was on the surface. Underneath it all, and not very far underneath it either, was the vivid memory of expelling an eight-pound child, whose head, I remain convinced, measured no less than three feet around, from an extremely delicate portion of my body. I was compelled to remind him of this fact at the slightest provocation, lest he forget.

And this was the easy part.

The difficulty lies in finding a way to respectfully negotiate the next eighteen years of parenting your bundle of joy. It can be difficult to be of one mind when confronted with the roughly eighty bazillion parental decisions we face on a day-to-day basis.

I remember watching a television program about multiples. For this couple, it was the father who, for the first few years, stayed home and cared for his quintuplets. Needless to say, he had a different style of parenting than I do. I was particularly intrigued by one part of his daily routine. The show followed him as he put the children down for their afternoon naps, after which he tidied the house, mopped the kitchen floor, and, in preparation for the afternoon snack, dumped an entire box of cheerios on its newly cleaned surface.

I was breathlessly relaying this to a friend on the phone, when I heard a chuckle from my husband.

"What?" I asked.

"I doubt very much," said the father of my children, "that he mops the floor every day."

Eeeeew.

Okay, so maybe we don't want to model ourselves too much on the male animal, given our fundamentally different understanding of such phrases as "balanced nutrition," "clean socks," and "adequate parenting"—not to mention their unwholesome desire for bacon and wide screen TVs and the vast stretches of their days dedicated to the subtle art of scratching themselves.

But odd as it may seem, after all these years, I no longer rail against these behaviors so different from my own. I have come to see a solid marriage and good parenting as a respectful balance of our differences—although I'm still holding out for a little less scratching.

I remember a small sledding party we hosted one winter. Three families, six kids, all at the time under the age of four. I had stayed behind with one of the mothers, while she nursed her newborn. We fully intended to meet the rest of the group at the park, but before we could bundle up, our fellow mother had returned. It seemed that the menfolk had decided that the best way to proceed, given the limited number of sleds, was to stack the children four deep on the back of a father and then hurtle the entire precariously balanced pack down the hill. My friend had rescued the youngest of the bunch and high-tailed it back to our house.

Needless to say, this is not how we mothers would have handled it.

One of my greatest sources of frustration as a mother is dedicating every waking moment to protecting my children from harm, only to have their father attempt to murder them at every turn. No mother has ever taught a child to swim by tossing him or her off a dock. No mother has ever condoned the building of a bike ramp. Fathers, on the other hand, will present their child (most likely their son) with a flimsy piece of plywood and an obviously insincere, "Be careful, now," then knowingly allow the child to pedal furiously down a hill and onto the plywood ramp before crashing to the hard, hard ground whereupon the father runs to the bleeding child and whispers, "Don't tell your mother."

The real bummer is that fathers may be right. Though I cannot help but wince at my husband's idea of "fun," I know that he is en-couraging our children's senses of curiosity and adventure, teaching them to be confident in the world. Which is great—if they survive.

As the kids have grown older, the stress has, if anything, increased. I used to worry myself into a state, terrified that I would drop them and somehow shatter that little soft spot on their heads or that their father would inadvertently feed them a grape or hot dog chunk that would prove their undoing. The world was rife with danger for these precious, soft, and vulnerable little beings, and I couldn't wait until they were a little bigger, a little tougher, so I could worry a bit less.

Ha.

My oldest is heading off to college soon, and my husband and I are terrified, *terrified*, that she is going to have to fend for herself. If anything, the stress has increased. Every unthinkingly boneheaded thing she does has Hubby and I shaking our heads, convinced that this, right here, is the kind of thing that will to lead to her living in our basement well into her thirties. And, frankly, maybe that's better for everyone.

Except that isn't right at all. You know it, Hubby knows it, and I, well, I mostly know it. I know that it may seem that those helicopter parents are the ones really putting themselves out, exerting the energy, but no. It is harder, much harder, to step back and let your clueless offspring loose on the world. Clueless because, although you have spoken until you are blue in the face and your vocal chords are sore, they appear to have retained not one bit of information you have tried to impart. (But let them come across you one night, giggling drunkenly with a girlfriend and surfing the Internet for pictures of Clive Owen and *that* they never forget. Selective memory, obviously.)

At least our parenting movement now has a name. A woman at work clued me in, and now I use it relentlessly: FIOWIO (Figure It Out, Walk It Off). Perfect.

Actually, now that I'm thinking of it, FIOWIO might be one of the few instances of patriarchal superiority in the realm of parenting. I'm sitting in the library, just now, watching two parents negotiate the weekly library trip with their offspring. The mom is trailing mere inches behind her brood, explaining, reading titles, shushing, while the dad is sitting waaaaaay on the other side of the library, resting in the biggest armchair he could find. He's not even reading a magazine. I think his eyes are closed. And guess what? Damned if his kids haven't picked out their books and checked them out first. Both of these parents successfully completed this common task, but only one of them managed to sneak in a nap.

Clap, clap, my hat is off to you, sir. As much as I hate it, I'm forced to think of all the times Hubby has planted his inert form solidly on the side of letting the kids do it themselves. Damned if he wasn't right all along. Please, for the love of God, do *not* tell him. That sort of admission requires a great deal of inner strength, and, frankly, I'm too dang tired to gracefully bow to the gloating. Maybe if I had been sneaking library naps all these years, it'd be a different story.

Given all these conflicts, it is common for women, at least the women I know, to develop crushes on men other than their husbands—men we do not actually have to live with. I, for one, had a deep and abiding love for our children's first pediatrician. I'm sure

:h the urge to protect our young. A man who could dispense antibiotics seemed ungodly sexy to me at n something as simple as describing the recommend- ed u⌒ ⁄ a particular antihistamine sparked distracting mental fantasies. I often ended up with no idea, exactly, of what to do for whichever child was ill, which prompted a follow-up call, which was, of course, no use at all. I could have left my husband take over, except for the aforementioned medical phobia. He, too, would have had no idea of what the doctor had said because he would have spent the entire appointment with his hands over his ears.

Besides, it was as close as I got to a date since the children's conception.

Alas, it was not to be. My eldest daughter announced during one of her yearly well-child checkups that I found his eyes "dreamy," necessitating a search for a new family physician, preferably female. Their immunizations haven't been up-to-date ever since. Although, oddly, Hubby is more inclined to squire the kids to appointments. Go figure.

Flirtations aside, I'd never leave my husband. At this point, he's got too much on me. He's the one person who has witnessed every humiliating, foolish, or incriminating thing I've done in the past two decades so, no matter how bad it gets, divorce is not an option. I'd have to kill him.

Just kidding. No cause for alarm or, say, a restraining order. I'm merely pointing to the larger picture here. Intimacy is born of proximity, and no one is closer to you than the man who shares your bathroom. He sees those little boxes of Nair and night cream. He's probably familiar with the scream that announces the arrival of another mutant chin hair. If he wanted to, he could reveal to friend or foe your dress size and the date of your last yeast infection. I don't know about you, but I find it safer all around to stay on my husband's good side.

Not that we don't have the same sort of dirt on our husbands. We do. It just doesn't amount to much leverage, that's all. His buddies could care less that his boxer shorts have a hole the size of a salad plate or that his towel smells like a wet dog. In fact, telling such secrets to your husband's friends actually elevates his status, as if questionable personal hygiene is proof positive of testosterone. Hell, it probably is. In short, we got nothin'.

Except this: My husband has a manly man job driving big trucks and operating heavy machinery with other manly men. I have heard enough stories directly from the horse's mouth to know that more often than you can possibly imagine, they kvetch, gossip, and moan about their relationships exactly as women do. I'm not quite sure why this information gladdens my heart, but it does. Despite their protests to the contrary, men are affected by their romantic relationships enough that they seek clandestine advice from other men. I know it. Now, you know it. It won't be long before they know that we know, and the balance of power will be restored.

No, that's not what I mean. Not really. Marriage shouldn't be viewed as a power struggle. As I said before, a good marriage is based on a respect for our differences—although sometimes "respect" is a little much to hope for. At times, we need to settle for a barely maintained tolerance. And for once, I'm not taking a jab at my husband. The incessant scratching notwithstanding, I willingly admit that I am, in fact, the more difficult one to live with. If my husband is a good-natured if somewhat gassy Irish setter, I am one of those nervous, yappy, hair-intensive breeds that needs to see a pet psychiatrist every time someone misplaces its favorite chew toy.

"How long have you been watching that game?" Yap! "Is that what you're eating for lunch?" Yap! "Do I look fat?" Yap! Yap! Yap!

I'm surprised he hasn't had me put down.

Thankfully, my husband has a generous nature and, recognizing that my intentions are good, tends to cut me a little slack. I think I just get caught in mommy mode, which is necessary for dealing with the kids but probably darn annoying for a spouse. I'm sure that when he left his parents' house, he thought his days of having to endure being told to button up his coat every time he stepped outside were over. Even I know that is ridiculous, though I seem incapable of stopping the words from pouring out of my mouth.

My only hope is to attempt to balance the incessant mothering with trying to give equal attention to our relationship as husband and wife. Okay, that right there was a total lie. Equal attention? Phfft. As if. At most I can offer him maybe one tenth of my brain space. In my defense, I am genetically hardwired to prioritize the health and well-being of my young. Also, there are just so many of them. The moment I walk in the door, I am swarmed and bombarded with requests. It's like dealing with my own diminutive paparazzi mob every time I come home from work. Hubby often will shoo them physically and loudly away from me, which he claims is his attempt to protect me from the children. Lately though, I've come to believe he is just using his larger stature to push his way to the front of the line. You'd think this boisterous outpouring of affection would gladden my heart, but mostly it tends to precipitate the beginnings of an anxiety attack.

So, what I'm saying is that it's difficult to turn around in the middle of the melee and focus, with any sort of real clarity, on my husband. Attempting to do so in our house is just foolhardy. Luckily, the kids are all getting older. So we are able, when not lying mute and exhausted on the couch, to sneak away to where the grown-ups are.

Miss Teen Wonder was so excited the day she finished her Red Cross babysitting certification. She ran into the house, brandishing her certification high in the air, and exclaimed, "Hey, look what I got!"

Unfortunately for her, she was playing to an empty house. Hubby and I were already hurrying down the sidewalk to the car. Holy sweet Jesus, that was one of my favorite days ever.

One of the first things we did was to take a yoga class together. It's pretty much what passed as "date night" in those days. What? It was totally legit. We wore special clothes; we had to drive across town; we spent an hour in a darkened room and were more relaxed when we left than when we started. See? Date night.

Plus, we enjoyed the added bonus of time to ourselves in the car. We had time to talk to each other without anyone yelling, "DAD, where are we going?" "MOM, tell him to get on his own side!" "I

AM!" "AM NOT!" until the main job of the spouse riding shotgun is to keep the driver from heading off a bridge.

I tell you, the car ride alone was worth the class fee.

Sometimes when we are floundering in challenges, we forget that we are really okay. One day we were having a discussion, a sort of "where are we now" overview of our lives, finances, the kids' school performances, etc., and Hubby says, "Well, no matter what else is going on, at least we know our relationship is good."

"Say what now?" I said.

"You and me. At least we're good."

And we were, so why did his comment surprise me? I guess I have a tendency to assume somewhere in my brain that when there is a challenge anywhere, it affects the whole system—like food dye in water.

With five kids, there is *always* a challenge; the law of averages means that at any given moment at least one (usually more) of the kids will be in some sort of trouble. Throw in a perpetually messy house, a dripping faucet, or a dying refrigerator and that frustration needs to come out somewhere. Underneath it all, I suspect that I'm the weakest link, and if I think that about me, why wouldn't he? Unfathomably, I am fortunate enough to be married to this completely delusional man, who thinks I am so much better than I know myself to be. Every time he tells me how special I am, I remind myself that it is time to check the furnace for leaks. Clearly, he has suffered some sort of trauma to the head, if only because of his insistence that I am one sexy lady. Ridiculous. I haven't shaved my legs above the knee in almost two decades, and, yes, I have, in a pinch, used shortening as a face cream, a beauty tip I read decades ago in one of my grandmother's magazines. Who knew the delicate odor of Crisco would be so intoxicating? I would be a fool to ever let this man go.

Eggnog vs. Firecrackers: Why Some Holidays Are Better than Others

While I love Christmas, there are other, lesser holidays that I find more than a little annoying. Presidents' Day, Columbus Day, all those noncelebratory occasions we have outgrown and whose only purpose seems to be to send the nation's parents scrambling to find weekday childcare due to school closings. Fourth of July is annoying, too. It's inevitably on a Tuesday, so I'm already bitter as hell about the sleep I'll be sorely missing the next day at work, and for what? To scramble for four square feet of lumpy, mosquito-infested hillside with every other family in the entire state, watch ten minutes, tops, of fireworks, then spend half an hour crawling around on my hands and knees in the dark, looking for my keys, or Hubby's wallet or the kid's iPod, before enduring the next forty-five minutes waiting to exit a parking lot. Tons of fun. Thank God the good people in my neighborhood have decided to ignore most city ordinances and have taken to setting off some serious fireworks in their backyards. Oh sure, there is the occasional maiming or house fire, but it's worth it to avoid the traffic.

If it were up to me, we'd only celebrate Thanksgiving, Christmas, New Year's DAY (Screw New Year's Eve. I don't celebrate anything that happens after 9:00 p.m.), and, of course, Mother's Day. Because I've earned it, that's why. Father's Day is totally unnecessary, from my experience, because I have yet to meet a father who will admit to wanting any sort of present and, as for the rest of the day's traditional activities—napping, watching sports on the TV, drinking beer, and probably grilling out—well, we have that already. It's called "Every Blessed Sunday."

The holiday I'm on the fence about is Halloween.

When kids are young, Halloween is so darn cute. Those angelic faces in those adorable costumes—it makes my heart ache just thinking about it. They are so excited and can't believe their mind-blowing good luck; they get to run around the neighborhood in full on dress-up clothes and their parents not only allow them but encourage them to accept candy from strangers. Candy! Plus, the little darlings have zero math skills, so if a fun-sized Snickers (or two or twenty) goes missing, who can prove a thing?

At this point in their young lives, they are irresistible. Yes, they are beautiful beyond belief in their donkey/ninja/truck stop waitress costumes, but it is their innocent enthusiasm that is most adorable. To them, the whole night seems enchanted, and they just cannot believe their good fortune to be born into such a time and place that would hold such magic as this.

On my son's first Halloween (the one where he actively walked himself, not was carried by Mom who ate all the candy "he" collected on the grounds that he was too young), Hubby sat on our front steps, passing out candy as SammyJ and I hit up the houses on the opposite side of the street. After every single house, our son would race to the sidewalk, brandish his plastic pumpkin full of loot, and whoop, "Daddy! They gave me candy!" And then hug it to his wee little chest.

Irresistible.

Flash forward a few years and the whole thing becomes a little shabbier, a little more jaded. It starts to feel like we're selling used cars in the oiliest of fashion. Innocent delight has been replaced by a deliberate and desperate mission to procure the most candy possible. I don't know about you, but once my kids started acting like deranged little junkies, the bloom was off the rose.

This Halloween we had a little more holiday excitement than normal. In short, the PoPo shut us down. Seems someone was lumbering around in an overcoat with a very realistic-looking gun. Realistic enough that the police drove through the neighborhood telling everyone that trick or treating was over, folks, head on in. Which of course we did, but I tell you what, I am 80 percent certain the threat was just some dumb-ass teenager on the lookout for free candy.

Teenage trick or treaters are the worst. Which is why we've instated the "no teenage trick or treating" rule in our house—a rule we've fudged a time or two through the years. "No teenage trick or treaters" eventually became "no middle school trick or treaters." It's just our bad luck that our youngest is also our wiliest and the least likely to let these sort of parental shenanigans pass. He's done the math and knows that entering kindergarten early is working against him. He has started an all-out campaign to make sure that he is not deprived of one lick of Halloween fun—not one fun-sized Snickers of it.

Teen-age trick or treaters have absolutely ruined the holiday for me, and though we can't stop other people from allowing their near-adult offspring to pilfer sugary treats from the neighbors, we can at least refrain from adding to the problem. Seriously, there are few things as unpleasant as having a sixteen-year-old clomp up to your door at nine thirty at night, long past the time when you care to be dealing with this so-called holiday fun anymore; ignore the universal signals of "I am done with this mess" (porch lights off and pumpkins extinguished); and beat on your door, begging for candy. Of course, he has no costume, nor holiday-themed treat bag. Just the biggest pillowcase he could find.

But these teenage extortionists are not the only guilty parties. They are abetted by parents who willingly drive them from neighborhood to neighborhood. Seriously? I hate those people. I want to stomp out to their cars and suggest that if they are so freaking desperate for candy, it'll all be half price in the morning. I'd be happy to float them the two bucks if they will just pack up their ginormous, sullen offspring and clear off.

While I may still be pondering the value of Halloween, I think I can say we are all on the same page when it comes to our other cherished holiday, and by that, I mean Mother's Day. You think I'm joking? My kids *love* Mother's Day.

Number one: I am the easiest person in the world to shop for. Five kids = five giant chocolate bars. Done.

Number two: Mother's Day is vastly unlike Father's Day, which is unanimously reviled by our children because of the fact that the only request their dad makes is that they spend the afternoon in his garden. I know. If I wasn't exempt because of an extremely forward-looking clause in our wedding vows, I'd hate Father's Day, too. As it stands, I'm rather fond of it. With the whole motley crew out of the house for the afternoon, I get to spend the day doing what I like best. Thus Father's Day becomes "Mom Hanging in the Basement, Drinking Merlot, and Watching Crappy Movies Day." I'd like to invite the kids to join me, but I can't afford the increase in the liquor budget. Who am I, Ernest Gallo?

Dad may want to spend his allotted day toiling away, but to me, that sounds a lot like normal, workaday drudgery. Nope, on Mother's Day, we eat out anywhere Mom wants to go, and then there is some sort of family outing. I'm still reaping the benefits of the year I unselfishly agreed to go to the laser tag, bumper car, video game place. Yup, that's me, unselfish like a fox.

Now we've settled into the nice Mother's Day ritual of a meal out and then a movie. It's really the only movie we see in the theaters together all year. Having five kids is nice and all, but prohibitive to any event or business charging more than a $2 admission. But I do love movies, and so, on Mother's Day we go. It makes this holiday one of my favorites of the year. I could get behind any holiday that involves a trip to the movies, even Halloween.

But the mother of all holidays is Christmas. I freaking love Christmas. At least I think I do. I never quite manage to pull off the whole gingerbread and peppermint cane wonderland I envision, but you can't help but love a holiday that encourages you to spike the eggnog. And right now, I need that little yuletide pick me up because Christmas is almost here.

Notice how mature I'm being and not fa-la-la-reaking out, despite the seemingly unavoidable slide into chaos that happens this time of year. Well, at least for me. Every November I think I am totally on top of this holiday thing. I finish my Christmas shopping before Thanksgiving and then toss the pile in a closet, as if someone else is going to sort, wrap, and mail those suckers. Ditto the cards. I get half-way through my address book and then run out of ink or time or the will to live and just sort of peter out.

Of course, I'm not behind on everything. I'm completely on schedule with my annual Christmas breakdown, in which I've reentered the wide-eyed world of the insomniac, caught a doozy of a cold that has knocked me flat on my butt for a week, and last night had to fess up to Hubby that my nightly mug of "tea" is really just cinnamon schnapps and hot water.

Don't judge. It's been a really stressful month.

Plus, Hubby and I just took on a joint part-time job, which is the best possible job we could have found, but still. Scheduling is starting to become a nightmare, and every time the kids try to change something on Mom's weekly calendar I run around the house with my hands over my ears yelling, "No backsies! No backsies!" Which doesn't make a lot of sense, now that I think about it.

Holidays ramp up the whole mess that is typical for our family. Holidays steal my time, and if I tried to throw money at the problem, the only thing that would shower down is dust. As a result, I spend an awful lot of time fretting and working myself into a decidedly nonjolly state.

Hubby is 100 percent no help at all. Every year he is on my "naughty" list before we even carve the Thanksgiving turkey. How such a sweet man can be such a Scrooge is beyond my comprehension. From the way he reacts you would think that he had a hidden, childhood holiday trauma—maybe spent a distant December 24th watching his orphanage burn to the ground or suffered a near fatal anaphylactic episode from a previously unknown allergy to candy canes. I swear to God, if he tells me one more time that we are going to "not go nuts and just have a little Christmas," I am going to clock him with the tree stand.

We have never "gone nuts." We have never had the resources to do so. Add to that his miserly approach to the holidays, I have never *once* gotten to do Christmas the way I want to. Not once! Besides, like every other working mother on the planet, I'm too dang beat to put the energy I'd like into transforming my house into a winter wonderland, and clearly, Hubby isn't about to help.

Every year, he fights the idea of getting a tree, since we're "just going to throw it out in a month anyhow." (Now you see why I spike the hell out of my eggnog?) I suppose there's a chance he may be joking, ho-ho-ho, but it is more likely his sadistic method of getting back at me for all the things I do that annoy him. Wait, nope, it can't be that. I'm pretty much perfect. Whatever his reasoning, it is unappreciated. I want a lovely Christmas. I want a jolly holiday filled with gingerbread and glitter and Bing Crosby carols. I do not want the same old, half-decorated, cat-decimated, grumpy husband debacle that we normally have.

I hope this is one of those situations where I am the only one who notices everything that is "wrong." I hope my kids think Christmas is the most magical holiday ever, never mind the messy house and Mommy crying in her bedroom. Who's to say that they even want the winter wonderland home or the Christmas dinner or the relentlessly cheerful carols. After all, they always get the one thing that is sure to set their little hearts aglow: presents.

Could it be that the excitement of the childhood Christmases that I remember so clearly and strive to recreate year after year comes down to plain old greed? Having watched my own children all these years, I have to admit to the possibility. I mean, placing presents under the tree, and then telling the kids, "These are for you but you *can't have them* until Christmas," well, isn't that pretty much like teasing a dog with a chew toy? Pretty soon they're spinning in circles, wild-eyed and foaming.

So maybe Hubby is right, at least as far as the kids are concerned. But that doesn't mean holidays are useless. Years from now, the kids will not remember that special present that set their greedy little hearts racing, but they will, if we're lucky, bring to mind memories of being warm and loved and full of cookies and content. It works for me, every dang year.

For example, recently, I was having just a hell of a day. I was coming off of a hormonally induced and barely repressed forty-eight hours of rage. The kind where on the outside I look pretty much normal, but on the inside I am a bottle of bubbling anger, just waiting for someone to pop that champagne cork of doom. And when they do? Imagine a soda can in a paint mixer—Ka-BOOM—a veritable geyser of obscenities and spittle.

This was my state of mind as I sat in my car in line at the car wash, minding my own business, which mostly involves taking deep, supposedly calming breaths and repeating an appropriate mantra ("Homicide leads to prison . . . Homicide leads to prison . . ."). Twenty-five minutes later, the door finally rises. Hurrah, my turn at last. Except the woman ahead of me is one of those who parks herself under the air dryer, hoping to extract every last droplet of water from the surface of her vehicle.

Now, I appreciate that this may have some merit in the dead of winter—you don't want to take the chance of your door or keyhole freezing shut—but it was forty-four degrees that day. Pardon me for saying so, but come the hell on! Just move the crappy Corolla already. I swear to God, if I had had a smaller deductible on my car insurance, I would have plowed through the car wash at forty miles an hour and pushed her Corolla out, Mad Max style.

Ka-BOOM.

Instead, I gave an exasperated yell, smacked my head in frustration against the steering wheel, and inadvertently changed the channel on the radio. That's when the Christmas miracle happened.

Tony Bennett started crooning "Silver Bells" from the stereo and I just . . . relaxed.

I react to Christmas carols much like Pavlov's dogs responded to bells. Deep, deep in the core of my brain, the opening strains of "The Twelve Days of Christmas" mean something good is going to happen (especially if it's the Muppets doing the singing). I have forty-five years of associating "Feliz Navidad" with good food, yummy smells, fun times with family, and presents. Not even an idiot in a soaking wet Corolla can interfere with that wiring. I've been working on those neuro-pathways since I was a baby. Forget deep breathing. Four bars of "O Holy Night" will send the stress leaking out of my toes.

How nice to find out that this is true, even when life hands you some significant changes. We're missing some much loved family members this year, and I wasn't sure I was going to be able to dig up much holiday spirit. But that was before Tony Bennett tapped into the well-spring of conditioned responses in my brain. If we're lucky, life is long and we have so many, many memories to draw upon. We never celebrate just one Christmas. Each year, we are marking and remembering and living the expression of all of them: the one when Grandma and Grandpa gave me a pair of pearl earrings; all the years Mom let us eat the entire, foot-long Santa Claus cookie after dinner and I was so full I had to lie on the floor to finish it; the first year with a baby; the year Kirk and his dad set the turkey on fire. The first year without Grandpa. Without Grandma.

Every year adds another memory to the day, another ornament to the tree. This is the first year Miss Teen Wonder, now a college student and arguably an adult, must travel home for the holidays. Her siblings will follow someday, one after the other, and with any luck, someday there will be grandbabies. (Do you hear me, children? LOTS of grandbabies.) Each holiday will be different than the last, with a rotating cast of loves gained and lost, different circumstances, different trees.

And I will celebrate them all. Because even though I am with my almost-grown children this year, they magically remain every age they ever were. They are still the same footie-pajama-clad children, struggling against sleep, straining to hear footsteps on the roof. And more miraculously, so am I, even if I seem to be nothing more remarkable than a middle-aged woman singing along to the radio in a car wash.

What? Me Worry?

I don't know how you approach birthdays, but as for me, I'm always working toward the next significant date. When I was twenty, I was looking forward to being twenty-five. At twenty-five I had my eye on thirty. In this manner, now that I am forty-six, I find myself contemplating fifty. I have to tell you, this is the first one that seems really, really big. FIFTY is going to be a deal.

So Hubby and I were in the car the other day, and I say to him, "I've been thinking about turning fifty. It seems pretty significant. It's been making me want to be very deliberate about how I'm going to spend the next fifty years."

Hubby snorted.

"What?" I said.

"The next fifty?" he inquired, his tone snarky enough to give the resident teenagers a run for their money.

"Yes, the next fifty," I said, deciding to ignore the general impertinence of the guy. Because I am mature and magnanimous that way, obviously. "I have been thinking about how I want to interact with the world. I really want to be more thoughtful about choosing to focus on the positive for the second half of my life."

"Half?" he hooted. "You are hilarious."

"You know what? I am going to live to be one hundred years old, dammit. I take excellent care of myself. I have the stout constitution of a German peasant. Oh, sure, I've never actually used sunscreen, the artificial sweeteners in my Diet Coke aren't doing me any favors, and perhaps I drink a little more wine than is strictly recommended, but so what? Shut up, you."

Hubby chortled, although given that he is a year older than I, I don't know what he found so damn funny.

"You know what," he said, "I'm glad you're thinking about it. You can be kind of pessimistic, you know."

I narrowed my eyes. "Well, given the tone of this conversation, I'm not too terribly optimistic of your chances right now."

It's weird to be lectured on optimism by a man who is at that moment telling me that I probably won't live nearly as long as I think I will. Am I right? Besides, much of what he calls pessimism, I would argue is just good common sense.

Case in point: his recent run-in with a car. Hubby optimistically believes that folks operating motor vehicles will, in fact, yield to pedestrians and cyclists, as is the law. Because of this misplaced optimism, he is forever striding right into the face of oncoming traffic, which wouldn't be so bad, except for the fact that he is often instructing the children to do the same thing. Scamper, children! Scamper into the street! You have the Right of Way. This is how he ended up getting T-boned by an SUV, while on his bike, in a crosswalk, right under a sign that said, "State law: yield to pedestrians and cyclists." Now who could have foreseen that?

Oh, right, me.

He will tell you that is my negativity talking, which is not in the least bit true. I am not being negative about the behavior of drivers. When it comes to automobiles, I am quite positive. I am positive that 80 percent of drivers are idiots 90 percent of the time. I'm 100 percent positive that they will not, in fact, yield to a cyclist or walker. One of us is right. I would argue that it is the person who was *not* struck by a motorized vehicle.

In some areas, Hubby is right. I do take a more pessimistic view of some things, little things, such as basic human nature.

Here's the thing: He's a history buff, which means he tends to take the long view. He sees the fact that we no longer consider pitting political prisoners against lions to be appropriate entertainment as proof positive that we are evolving into kinder beings. I form my opinions using a somewhat more immediate view, believing, for example, that the ongoing media presence of Donald Trump proves we are ignorant boobs who get what we have coming to us.

Lately, he is starting to freak me out. He has focused his natural inclination to track potential newsworthy trends on the End of Cheap Oil (cue the cackle of crows and ominous music). Every day he finds new evidence that we have tapped out our global oil supplies. Oil futures remain flat, he mentions. China has stopped subsidizing gasoline for its citizens, and there has been no subsequent drop in price per barrel. Oil industry spokespersons confirm that oil fields are operating at perhaps 90–80 percent of their peak rates. He will *not* stop telling me these things, despite my increasingly desperate pleas. To him, this is fascinating. To me, it's end times.

So maybe I watched too many science fiction movies back in the day, but I know what the future looks like once oil is gone and the masses no longer have access to Mocha Venti Lattes and cheap electronics. It's going to get *allllll* Mad Max up in here. You mark my words. We are not going to transition well. Hubby thinks it's will be interesting from an academic point of view, but that's because he mistakenly thinks we're higher up this food chain than we are. I've got news for you, honey, we're grunts. We are going to end up living with the mutant hookers in that slum town from the movie *Total Recall*, which is *not* the life I envisioned for our children.

All of this End of Cheap Oil talk has turned Hubby into a sustainability freak. He rides his bike to work, even in the winter (until recently, that is). He talks about owning land—and sheep.

Me? I'm going a different route. When he gestures at the city and says, "All this is going to change." I have the immediate urge to run out and start stockpiling coffee, chocolate, and pretty shoes—none of which are indigenous to Minnesota. (We have soybeans, sugar beets, and Red Wing Work Boots.) I can't imagine that when the oil is gone, shipping cocoa nibs up to the frozen north is going to be a huge priority to anyone but me.

Hubby has me so on edge that I'm one hot second away from wearing a "The End is Near!" sandwich board. Just today I pulled into the liquor store and noticed that there was not a single car in the parking lot. It struck me as eerily odd, bordering on sinister. Think about it. When was the last time you saw an empty liquor store parking lot?

"Are we under attack?" I thought to myself, then laughed. Silly me. If something truly catastrophic happened, the *first* place we'd all head for is the liquor store. At least I would, quickly, before the lines of distribution for all that sweet, sweet wine dried up. The second thing I'd do is loot all the chocolate I could find. Same reason. Thirdly, because I'd be morally and legally obligated, I'd gather up the kids from school. Oh sure, they might be mad about the delay at first, but later, when we are all living underground, because sentient robots have taken over the surface, and we have the last remaining stores of fun-size Snickers, they'll thank me.

(Don't even ask us to share. We don't know you. You should've thought about that when you were racing around, gathering your children and filling the bathtubs with clean water. Phfft, *water*.)

And once the oil goes you can forget about Christmas, beautiful Christmas, the best day of the year. Once Amazon.com stops shipping sweaters and DVDs, Christmas is going to be Little House on the Prairie style lame. You're gonna wish Santa gave you coal, nice, combustible coal. As it is, we'll be sitting around our makeshift wood stoves, burning bits of furniture we looted from the deserted Sharper Image store, drinking homemade sugar beet wine, and reminiscing about Norelco electric razors and Chia Pets.

At least you will. I'll be locked in my room, eating chocolate from my sock drawer stash. When I'm not sharpening sticks into pointy-ended spears, that is. Maybe that speaks to a lack of trust on a basic level, but I prefer to think of it as being prepared.

As much as it pains me to admit it whenever Hubby is right, I do tend to worry more than is technically necessary, and not just about the future lack of oil. Case in point: Every day since Hubby left his previous job to pursue a new career, I have worried about our finances. Every single day. And do you know what has happened? Nothing. We've made a few adjustments, but we are in exactly the same financial shape as we were before. Sure, it's not like there's a ton of home renovation happening around our place and our financial planning largely consists of me periodically bursting into the family room, looking at our three daughters, and bellowing, "We are *not* paying for your weddings!" But we have no huge debts, no creditors beating down our door, nothing.

Life is short, and maybe it's best not to spend time worrying about all the little stuff that I usually spend my time obsessing over. With that in mind, I've given myself permission to just relax, for the love of Pete; to just take a breath and enjoy the day ahead.

In an effort to transform my innate, German pessimism into something a tad more cheerful, I have made a list of things I am no longer going to waste time worrying about:

1. Grocery bills. I have a sixteen-year-old son who wears size twelve men's shoes. I need fifty dollars a week just to keep him in generic cereal. The days of our eighty-dollar-per-week food budget are over. Fuggetaboutit.

2. The sorry state of my marathon race photos. I am no longer going to lament the fact that the photos taken during my races do not show the lithe and leggy runner of my dreams but rather a red-faced, middle-aged woman with terrible posture and a clear need for medical attention. Dammit.

3. The electronic ruination of our youth. That's right, children. Talk on your stupid phones nonstop. Text and tweet so continuously that you forget how to speak to another human being face to face. Go ahead and get a chip implanted in your brain so you can stream YouTube directly into your cerebral cortex twenty-four hours a day. Reenact *WALL-E* in real

time. I'll be at the library checking out actual *books*. Because I am old, that's why.

4. Finding the perfect summer purse. I have sixteen purses, and they are all wrong. I suppose it's not the worst thing in the world, is it?

5. The state of my saggy, old lady behind. Since I can't even see it, I consider it more your problem than mine.

6. Having my optic nerve eaten away by the artificial sweeteners in my beloved diet soda. This is a rumor I heard once in high school and think about every time I drink a soda. At the time, I was also very concerned about the existence of Big Foot, alien abductions, and the Bermuda Triangle. This is what happens when your primary source of information was your grandmother's *Weekly World News* magazine.

7. That one guy who always wants to sit with me on the bus. He's probably either a) lonely or b) a little socially awkward and not c) a serial killer. Let's hope.

So far the ramifications of my efforts have been good. I've spent far more time hanging with my kids and much less time worrying about whether the ever-growing pile of half-empty paint cans in my basement will one day explode or that my impromptu haircut makes me look like Sigourney Weaver in *Alien* on some days and Nancy Reagan on others.

If I had to be honest, I suppose I could admit that I am a girl of conflicting motivations. You would think that someone who worries as much as I do would be a strictly organized and regimented sort, that I would attack the uncertainty of this life with some good, solid planning.

You would be wrong.

When laying out a framework for my future, I have always tended to be more spontaneous than one would think. Well, spontaneous or lazy, depending on the generosity of your definition. The flip side of my perception of the Universe as a capricious and unknowable ball of chaos is the tiny sliver of hope that something really cool could happen, something unpredictable that I would miss if I marched lock-step and head-down a certain path. It's a good exercise in optimism, but hell on my sense of security. Had I made some sort of rational plan for my life certain aspects of it would be much, much different and no doubt easier. There would have been some sort of structured ascent, career-wise (heck, there would have been some sort of actual "career"), and perhaps a financial pay-off that involves neither a small claims lawsuit nor a tiny man in a green suit leading me to his pot of gold.

My mom, fresh out of a retirement seminar, called recently to sound the alarm about what the future holds. "You know," she said, allegedly helpfully, "by the time you retire, you are going to need a minimum of a million dollars."

I snorted. "Well, I'm not going to have it."

"But you need it."

"But I'm not going to have it."

"I'm serious."

"*I'm* serious."

So there we were, dead in the water, locked in the conversational equivalent of a *High Noon* stand-off. Unfortunately for both of us, my only goals have revolved around the type of person I want to be and not a desire to, you know, eat actual people food in my twilight years. I'm sure all that personal growth will be a great comfort to me when I'm mopping the floor at McDonald's in my nineties.

Money is the source of 80 percent of my worrying. Hubby does not share my apprehension about our financial security. He believes that the best approach to money is to be cheerfully nonchalant about the whole thing.

"Money means nothing," he says. "What's important is your family, your loved ones, and living according to your values."

What a lunatic.

The kids love it when he gets in these moods because it means that he is about make a grand gesture intended to either a) cheer me up or b) teach me a lesson in how to *not* be a money-hoarding, nail-biting train wreck—like the time Hubby and I finally joined the new millennium and broke down and bought a Wii.

We told the kids that they couldn't play it until the house was spotless. And, honey, Momma didn't lift one dang finger to help. Every once in a while, I'd meander into a room, wave my coffee cup vaguely over the domicile, and offer helpful suggestions such as, "Don't forget to dust" and "Did you clean under the bed?" That Wii was the most fun I'd had in ages, and we hadn't even cracked the seal on a game yet.

Of course, the Wii turned out to be a pain in my tuchas. We surprised the kids. While out running errands, we grabbed the whole darn system, three extra games, chargers, extra remotes. Watching their notoriously cheap parents act with such abandon must have renewed our children's faith in miracles and the power of prayer. And trust me, they had been praying mightily—and whiningly ("Pleeeeeze, can we have a Wii? Pretty pleeeeeze)—for that gaming thing for a while.

It was all going swimmingly. Their little faces were all aglow, Mom and Dad for once were the heroes of the hour, peace and love reigned—then our check was denied. Which is just the sort of thing Hubby was trying to demonstrate to me that I shouldn't be worried about.

Mortified, we called the bank and were informed that as we had not established a history of writing large checks (see aforementioned cheapness), the bank could not approve the sale.

"But we have the money," I said, reasonably.

"Yes."

"But I can't have it?"

The woman on the line paused. "You may have $100."

Wow. One hundred bucks of my very own money. Thanks. Suddenly, our credit union had decided to act as if I were a drunk and unstable pop star and assume conservatorship over my finances. And the thing is, the Wii is hardly the worst financial decision I ever made. Where was the bank when I spent the bulk of my college tuition money on spiral perms and Doc Martins, hmm? If ever I resembled a tipsy pop star, it would've been college, not now. And how about the time we bought a used car and unbeknownst to us, the frame had completely rusted through to the point that the darn thing *split apart* as I was driving it not two weeks later. I wouldn't have minded a bit if someone would have stopped that sale. But *no*. Attempting to purchase a lousy gaming console gets us denied. It was like having your allowance suspended from Mom and Dad.

In the end, we used our credit card and slunk from the store. And in truth, the kids didn't care how we got it, just that we did. And there were no financial repercussions; we still paid our bills that month, and we still have the cushion in our checking account. (Maybe someday our bank will even let us use it.) In short, nothing terrible happened so maybe Hubby was right and I can cross money off my worry list. Although it will be difficult to overcome my normal tendency to worry, at least I have plenty of time to practice—fifty years, I reckon, sixty on the outside.

Meant to Be

Sometimes, it is good to practice letting the Universe take care of things by setting out on an endeavor that is so mind-bogglingly huge that even your stubborn, untrusting soul must concede the need for divine intervention. Twice I have managed to joyfully stand back and let nature take its course, confident that the outcome would prove the most perfect of all possible results. The first was when Hubby and I decided to get married. Even though it took us two and a half years to actually pull off any sort of ceremony (that's what you call "playing the long game"); even though we didn't think much about the décor at our reception, which was held at a German beer hall which the staff had recently decorated for Halloween; and even though I spent the day before my wedding looking for something, anything, to wear because apparently when you enter your second trimester, some of your clothes no longer fit—none of that mattered. All in all, it was the most perfect day of my life, thus far. All of my friends drank far too much beer, sang drinking songs at the top of their voices, and danced enthusiastic, sloppy polkas—even my uncles. (They had disappeared after the service but resurfaced a few hours later. Mysterious? Not really. Apparently, I also forgot maybe the most important thing in all of Wisconsin during the fall, which is not to schedule your wedding reception during a Packers game.)

The second time I let the Universe run with the ball was when Hubby and I decided that, since we hadn't messed up our first two children too terribly, we were prime candidates for becoming adoptive parents. Normally, when embarking on any course of action, my mind is a jumble of indecision and self-doubt. Figuring out what to cook for supper can take me all afternoon. Deciding whether or not to join a gym requires a complex analysis of finances, scheduling, and self-reflection of such intensity that one would think I was attempting to resolve once and for all, all of life's deepest questions: "Is there a God?" "Does my life have a purpose?" and "Who ate all the trail mix? Seriously. I just bought a new bag, like, two days ago."

Adoption, however, for some mysterious reason, seemed like a no-brainer. And by that I mean, my brain absolutely refused to get involved. I had no notions on what my future children might be like or look like or how they would fit into our family. I felt no need to torture myself, attempting to imagine the potential twists and turns of this journey. I was swaddled in the certainty of the rightness of our actions. I've truly spent more time weighing the pros and cons of donning a particular pair of jeans, than I did on whether or not to expand our family in this way. To this day, I have no idea why that was true. It just seemed inevitable that it would happen.

For a while, Hubby was in the dark about this unlikely turn of events. He felt, much more keenly than I, the tremendous change we were about to undertake. He agonized over the possible ramifications of our actions and the effect we would be having on these vulnerable young charges. "What are you thinking?" he demanded. "What are your worries? Your concerns? What are you hoping for? Are you at all afraid?"

I gave him a wan smile. "Honestly, sweetie, whenever I try to think about it . . ." (and here I shrugged) "all I hear in my brain is white noise. Nothing."

Hubby immediately called our social worker and declared a hiatus. To him, my uncharacteristic calm was downright spooky and evidence that maybe the enormity of our decision had caused my mind to snap once and for all. He was not about to enter into this process with an abnormally serene partner who responded to his heart-felt and increasingly frenetic queries with the clear-eyed and unquestioning smile of a simpleton. It took three months before he was convinced that my utter certainty was due to an unwavering commitment to adoption and not an undiagnosed mental break.

Hubby wasn't the only one who found my equanimity unusual. Mary, our social worker, was accustomed to the frantic calls and inquiries of couples who have experienced tremendous trials in their quest to have a family. Often adoption is an avenue they come to after other options have failed. More than once, I felt terribly self-conscious in a group of prospective adoptive parents, apologetically confessing that we already had two healthy, biological kids at home, an embarrassing and unfair display of good fortune.

Mary would sometimes call, warning us that we would be unable to reach her for a spell due to the need to escort children to their new homes, but breathlessly promising to call us the very day she returned to the office.

"Mary, don't worry about it," I would say. "Take a day or two to get your bearings. Call us when you're caught up."

There would be dead silence on the other end of the line, then a tentative, "Are you sure?"

"Positive," I'd say, hoping that our lack of urgency wasn't being misinterpreted as disinterest.

Happily, this rare display of calm proved justified. Events came together in a way utterly supporting my belief that we are not floundering about on our own; that help is on the way and maybe sometimes life has something in store for us that we, even as clever as we are, didn't see coming.

Hubby and I finished the roughly eight million pages of paperwork from the adoption agency, the worst of which was the checklist of acceptable health conditions for our future child. You learn a lot about yourself when you are picking and choosing your way down a checklist of possible afflictions: Club foot, okay. Fetal alcohol syndrome, no. Partial blindness, okay. Total blindness, um, okay? No, wait . . ." That was a level of self-assessment I would rather have skipped.

While we waited for a referral, we were granted access to the Waiting Child website, which is basically a gathering house for older children, children with medical concerns, and sibling groups. Determined to let the Universe bring me my perfect child, I swore to never look at it.

Unfortunately, the Universe refuses to ever follow my preferred schedule. I waited what I thought was a reasonable amount of time, and then twice that, before I finally broke down and scrolled through the heart-tugging photos on Waiting Child. There, among all the darlings, was a picture of what we thought were twin brothers and their little sister, ages three and one, from Ethiopia. They all stared, unsmiling and untrusting into the camera, so protective of each other and so beautiful.

My heart lurched into my throat. I swallowed hard and shook my head to clear the tears from my eyes. "Ridiculous," I admonished myself sternly, "we are not adopting three children." Then I printed out their photo.

"Ridiculous," said my husband, when I silently handed it to him, "we are not adopting three children."

"Absolutely not," I agreed.

The next morning, when I woke, Hubby was sitting next to the bed, photo in hand. "Call Mary," he said.

"Ridiculous," I responded as I sprinted to the phone.

Mary was silent for a second, after I told her that we really wanted to adopt the sibling group from Ethiopia. She put me on speaker and made me repeat it, loudly, so her coworker heard. They both started whooping and laughing but not saying much to yours truly, which wasn't great for my poor, jangled nerves.

"Mary has lost it," I reported to my husband. "We are going to need a new social worker."

But we didn't. Mary was celebrating like crazy because she was privy to additional information. "That referral showed up on my desk two days ago with your name on it," she said. "I turned it down and told them that you were *not* adopting three kids."

"Ridiculous," I said, beaming.

We didn't know it at the time, but Mary was struggling through the final stages of cancer. It had to be reassuring to see evidence of a larger force at work, some small suggestion that there is a plan for us, after all. I like to think so, even though there is blessed little evidence of it on a daily basis.

Some time later, as we were waiting on approval from the Ethiopian government for our twin girls and their little brother (So sorry, Little Man. How were we to know that Ethiopians dress their little boys in pink? Also, you were just so very, very pretty.), we were approached by a woman at our church. Surprisingly, given the small size of our congregation, we had never met. As it turned out, she had been informed by another member about our pending adoption. This struck her as odd, as she was the very person in charge of all overseas adoptions in our city and had no recollection of seeing our file. She reported that she had undertaken a thorough search and located our application, languishing in the never-land of Homeland Security, due to a clerical error. Without that one, off-the-cuff comment, who knows how long we would have had to wait? If we weren't members of the same church, she probably wouldn't have felt the compulsion to locate our file and personally keep tabs on the process or to contact us with all sorts of good advice.

"Make copies of everything," she'd admonish, "EVERYthing! I'm sending you copies right now. Notarize them. Take them with you."

At the time, I thought she was being a bit paranoid but later discovered she was a genius. Her advice saved us when I was standing at the counter of the Ethiopian consulate in Addis Ababa, nose-to-nose with a clerk who told me, sorry, they had absolutely no records of me, my family, or my intention to take the three children clustered about my ankles anywhere.

"Would this help?" I asked, and pulled from my bag a stack of paperwork roughly the same density as books four through seven of the *Harry Potter* series. Our new friend had so instilled in my brain the absolute importance of these papers that I had been carrying them on my person since the morning we left for the airport. And lucky thing, too. Our luggage had gone missing somewhere between Washington, DC and Rome. Unaccustomed to international travel, I foolishly assumed my bags would arrive with me. In my carry-on, I had no change of clothes, no toothbrush, no emergency underwear. I had none of the gifts I'd carefully chosen for the children. No cell phone. I'd been bumping around Ethiopia with my wallet, six magazines (four *People* and two *InStyle*), an empty Snickers wrapper, and—halleluiah!—my gigantic file folder of copies. I let it fall to the counter with a satisfying "thud" and returned to my seat, smiling, to wait while the clerks angrily hashed it out among themselves. When we were finally summoned to return to the counter, we were told that even though it was highly unusual, they would accept my files and use them to finish processing the kids' visas. Of course, they would. Given that the entire Universe was behind me, how could they do anything else?

These days, there are times when I find myself anxious, angry, conflicted, and plagued with self-doubt, and the suspicion surfaces that I have ruined any chances for Mother of the Year. There are times when I think that child protective services probably should be alerted as to the extreme ineptitude of my parenting. One or more of the children is making me quite insane, I feel, and if it is any of our three youngest, the pain is multiplied by a hundred, at best. My biological kids, let it be said, take after my side of the family. Sorry, honey, they just do. The snarky, dark humor. The too-loud voices. The love of stupid movies and bad puns. That's all me. They are familiar to me in all the snakey, sneaky ways DNA passes on our best and worst traits. When I am yelling at them in all my maternal fearsomeness, I do not second-guess my instincts. "I know what you are up to!" I bellow, and I do.

Besso, Tigist, and Miki are different. We had to form our family, learn to draw toward each other. I cannot predict their responses with the same certainty as I can with someone who has my same cowlicks and love of banana taffy. Sometimes when I am scratching my head over their inexplicable behavior, I think I am maybe the worst person with whom they could have ended up. So many times, I feel that I am falling short of being the perfect mother I would wish for them. I think that maybe there is a better match somewhere; a parent who is no doubt a hundred times nicer and more patient and cuddlier than I am. I think about this, and then I remember the miraculous way they came to be ours.

"Ridiculous," I tell myself and get back to the business of being a family.

This Is the Chapter in Which I Save the Baby Chicks and Annoy My Children Beyond All Measure

Given my tendency for seeking self-improvement, my focus on food—what we are eating, is it healthy, is it cheap, is it too toast intensive (answer: yes)—is probably predictable. Like nearly every other American female, I spend far too much time thinking about food. In this situation, though, I don't know how I can get around it. Trying to keep this crew in peanut butter crackers is hard enough, but cooking for seven people is just plain exhausting. I love to eat good food, though, and since the children consume my financial resources just as quickly as they do an open box of cereal, I do not have the option of frequenting fine restaurants. I have to prepare it myself.

I wouldn't mind cooking every blessed meal, if my children didn't share so many opinions about it. And believe me, there is no one as committed to sharing as a ten-year-old with an opinion. Let me begin with this: I am an excellent cook. I do not need any input about the choice of pasta sauce, the texture of the vegetables, or whether or not fruit constitutes "dessert." (In this case, the kids are right. It absolutely does not. But it is healthier and gets me out of the kitchen a half-hour sooner, so too bad, my darlings. So sorry about your excellent health and lack of childhood diabetes. I'm the worst.)

I do not, in fact, need any input at all. Every week, I plan the entire week's menu, taking into account work and school schedules, personal preferences, and our budget. It is an excruciating process, and successfully maneuvering the logistics and quirks of our many-membered household should qualify me for some sort of high-stakes, sensory overload career such as air traffic controller or NASCAR superstar.

But, no, all it qualifies me for is work in a dank basement somewhere, dealing with customer complaints. Because I sure get a lot of them. This one prefers Alfredo sauce to marinara; that one thinks we should have more onions in the stir fry; someone else thinks onions are gross. (Oh, wait, that's me.) And virtually everyone laments our lack of packaged snack foods.

How fabulous would it be to have someone provide food for you *every single day*? Doesn't that sound just wonderful? And it isn't just food, is it? It's food and clean clothes and new underpants and fresh notebooks. Oh my God, it sounds just like heaven. Well, it does to a grown-up anyway. To children, it sounds like torture. Food they don't like, clothes they didn't select, notebooks for a school that they don't want to attend in the first place.

When I tell them they will never have it as good as they do right now, they roll their eyes. They sit there, night after night, hating the broccoli or the potatoes or some other such nonsense. They thought they were just stating their preferences, when in reality they were digging their graves.

Yup, since they were going to complain incessantly anyway, I decided that I might as well go for broke—and become a vegan. Now, they *long* for the days they could complain about my meaty chili or chicken pot pie. Now, if they want to complain about the food they are eating, chances are they don't even know what it is.

In truth, this all started as an attempt to eat healthier and maybe lose a few pounds, an objective that completely backfired. I am perhaps the only person to convert to a vegan diet and promptly gain ten pounds. This makes me either the best or worst vegan ever, I'm not sure which. In any case, I think we can all agree that I am decidedly enthusiastic. I happen to like avocados, cashews, and fried tofu more than cheeseburgers or sausage. The kids do not. That plaintive and mysterious wail you hear around six thirty every evening? That's my children responding to my announcement that I have found another new recipe for lentil loaf.

This gives me a perverse and profound joy. The more they complain, the more I dig my heels in and cackle.

Besides, I'm not technically making them eat anything. In addition to my own stash of vegan burgers and nut spreads, I still buy cheese and eggs and milk and meat. They are welcome to prepare whatever they would like. So far, though, their laziness has triumphed over any culinary objections. Simply put, they are so accustomed to food magically appearing before them that they can't even consider conjuring up some of their own. It's as if the muscles that would allow them to power through the kitchen and open the refrigerator door have somehow atrophied. Which is funny, because put a pan of brownies in the fridge—vegan or no—and they seem to be able to get to it just fine. So really, they are not suffering from weakness brought on by extreme anemia, as they might claim; they are suffering merely from a lack of imagination.

They get it from their father.

For years, Hubby has looked at me helplessly when I have tried to elicit input on what he would prefer for dinner. Opening the refrigerator wide and examining the contents, he cries in frustration, "It's all just ingredients!" by which he means, not *food*, not something he could possibly assemble into a collection of potential dishes via the complex imagining of his brain. This is why my family needs to keep me around. The lot of them would starve to death without me. The authorities would find their inert forms, crouched around a pile of foodstuffs, maybe holding a potato in one hand, a puzzled look etched on their faces for all eternity.

Yeah, they'll eat vegan food. They'll eat it and *like* it.

No, they'll hate it but only on principle. Only because arguing with me is the way that they siphon all the youth and enthusiasm from my body and use it to propel themselves through their day. They ate bean burritos a hundred thousand times before I started toying with this new lifestyle. It was a standard, and much loved, weeknight meal. Now that I'm cooking vegan, we're back to those opinions. The tide has turned, and, apparently, bean burritos are now bad, very bad.

I've tried stealth; for a while, I wasn't telling anyone what they were eating or what alterations I had made to the food. If they asked I'd give a casual shrug, and say, "Chocolate cream pie." The problem was, I couldn't keep information to myself. When they asked for seconds, I would play it super-casual, "Oh, you like that?" And then when they said yes, I would pounce, "Ha! The secret ingredient is TOFU, suckers!"

Now, every time I make something particularly appealing, they sniff it, narrow their eyes, and ask (not unreasonably), "What is it, really?" (Answer: most often, chickpeas.)

Hubby is 100 percent behind my attempt at veganism. In fact, he's oddly supportive. When I asked him why, he put forth the theory that, with all the healthy eating going on around our place, he will never have to take any sort of pill or endure any medical heart- or blood pressure-related procedures.

(Note: My husband is a big, whiny baby when it comes to blood or doctors or anything that might result in the most insubstantial perusal of one's, let us say, soft tissue. It was why when the kids had a loose tooth dangling by the barest thread of gum, I always sent them to him. Sure, he was absolutely no help at all, but it was *hilarious*.)

"You realize," I told him, "that to reap the benefits of my vegan diet, you actually have to join me in it."

Hubby disagreed; he maintained that he was getting all the fallout of the health benefits of my veganism.

He also is convinced that he has radically changed his diet as well. Since, during the time that he made this claim, I was eating a zucchini, mushroom, garlic, and olive pizza, hold the cheese, and he was eating a large slice of pepperoni, I question his analytical processing.

The previous evening, for example, we ate at a Chinese restaurant. I ordered tofu and vegetables in a spicy sauce. He ordered General Tso's chicken. The waiter gave him the option of sautéed skinless chicken or breaded and deep fried.

"Which is better?" Hubby asked me.

I raised an eyebrow, "Better for you? Or better tasting?"

Hubby laughed. "Fried," he said.

Again, I question his reasoning.

It's good that I'm going first into this endeavor, though. It is difficult enough to sell veganism without the lies that are habitually put forth by well-meaning but clearly delusional members of the lifestyle. Vegan foods do not taste the same as nonvegan foods. Soy milk does not taste like cow milk. No one who has tasted it would ever mistake vegan cheese for cheddar. There is a vegan scale of deliciousness ranging from almond ice cream sandwiches, which are delectable, to nutritional yeast, which is dreadful. Yet, for whatever reason, vegans are always encouraging the newly initiated to add nutritional yeast to their sauces to get that "cheesy" taste. Lies, all lies. The only thing nutritional yeast tastes like is wet goat, and I am speaking from bitter experience.

Happily, though, Oreos are vegan. Also pie and most dark European chocolates.

I might have just figured out why I gained those ten pounds.

No matter, I'm happier eating vegan foods, despite what the kids say. And what's the worst that can happen? The kids grow up eating a ton of veggies and legumes, however grudgingly, or they rebel and start cooking their own nonvegan meals. I win in either of those scenarios, so really, I couldn't care less. In the meantime, I'll just stick to the vegan game plan and wait to see how it all shakes out. Tonight's menu? "Cheesy" black bean and sweet potato enchiladas, spicy, with just the faintest hint of goat.

Mother Knows Best,
But Nobody Ever Listens

Sometimes, despite their firmly held belief that I am an idiot, my children manage to learn something from me. It's such a rare occurrence that I feel I have to revel in these small successes. Yesterday, for example, I managed to pass down a bit of wisdom to my son and convey a talent that I have honed through exhaustive practice and perfected through the bitter tears of experience.

Yesterday, I taught him how to shop online.

You laugh, but only because you do not realize how awesome I am at that task. If the Miss America Pageant had an online shopping category, Mario Lopez would be crowning my triumphant, yet elderly and chunky self while willowy wannabes wept copious, mascara tears in the background. I'm that good.

Our eldest son has expensive tastes. I could find him the most perfect and coveted teen dream item of clothing with the tags still on it, but if it happened, heaven forbid, to come from a thrift store? Fuggetaboutit. I'm considering keeping a stash of department store bags and receipts in the car. Just fold up those Goodwill jeans and tuck them in the "legitimate" bags. Deceptive? Sure. But he can't have these champagne tastes on our Skittles budget.

Heck, we can't even afford Skittles.

Luckily, the boy is also pragmatic. If he needs cash, he goes out and earns it. He and a friend spent one weekend knocking on doors to drum up a little yard-raking business. They raked our neighbor's lawn and then were plied with soda and leftover Halloween candy and paid triple their fee. I'm thinking about getting into the yard-raking business myself.

His money, however, is different than mine. Mine is apparently as plentiful as blades of grass and requires no more consideration. His? Well, his stash of green is precious and any expenditures must be carefully considered and prudently acted.

And that's a good thing. Half the battle of having money is saving money, so this is a good impulse on his part. He had in mind a certain pair of jeans, specific in hue and cut, the possession of which would no doubt catapult him to the highest echelon of the high school society. The material of these jeans must be spun from the finest webs of Amazonian spiders, to judge from the cost, but never fear. I am so darned skilled that not only did I find said jeans at far less than half the original price, but I found an online coupon that more than paid for shipping and netted him a free T-shirt in the bargain. Eldest Son hasn't looked at me with such pride in years.

There she is . . . Miss Amerrrrrica . . .

Maybe I'm a little overly excited, but I am committed to teaching my kids about money, if only because I'm so screwed up about it. On the one hand, money is 100 percent not important to me. I'm not impressed by big-ticket status items. On the other hand, the thought of not having enough (defined as "sufficient to get us through whatever unseen catastrophe might be looming just over the horizon") can send me rocking in a fetal position in the corner. This is *not* the monetary attitude I want my kids to have. I want them to be sensible and safe but not overly concerned when it comes to money. Because, really, who doesn't go through a roller coaster of circumstances in their lives? It is better to develop the equanimity needed to ride out the lows now, when the worst thing that could happen is you have to buy the generic bubblegum.

How to deal with money or, specifically, how to deal with those times in your life you lack money is something young couples probably should talk about before they get married. I don't think Hubby and I ever did. When we were young, we talked about which bar we were going to meet our friends at or which countries we wanted to travel to or the devastating breakup of the British indie band, The Smiths. We were too wrapped up in our invulnerable youth to think about the future. Besides which, we had no money to speak of, so the answer to the question of how we would deal with a lack of money would have been, "Pretty much exactly like this."

Luckily, we magically managed to be compatible in our lack of desire for money. Hubby more so than me, admittedly. He doesn't want a thing. He's too busy laying plans for the post-oil world he is certain is coming. Plus, he's rediscovered his childhood dream of being a rancher. Given that he's married to an avowed city girl and the only creatures around to herd are children, he has settled for gardening. As it turns out, he rather loves it. He spends hours plotting next year's garden, annexing more and more of the yard, and trying to convince me to let him keep bees (no).

The last thing that I need is for him to decide to go all hill-folk survivalist on me, no matter how bad it gets. I'm simply too old and too tired to learn to weave my own clothes. However, when the kids were younger and I was a stay-at-home mom, financial constraints necessitated that I be frugal. Beyond frugal. I was one car repair away from having to make my own soap in the backyard. I have to admit that I got a certain masochistic satisfaction from living on the edge. I knew three different ways to cut the colored paper handouts sent home from school into birthday streamers. I made my own Christmas gifts. I knew the per serving cost of every meal I cooked and could feed our family of seven on less than twenty dollars a day. Even though our allotted food budget has expanded, I still can. It's just that for medicinal purposes, Hubby and I now drink the surplus.

In an odd way, I had a much better attitude about money then. I approached our financial hardships with a "Chin up. Won't this be a jolly challenge?" mentality. So you'd think now that we have a modicum of financial stability I'd be perfectly calm and content.

That would be lovely. But no.

Every month, when it is time to pay the bills, I drag myself to the task looking for all the world like a French queen on her way to the gallows. Scratch that. I'm not at all noble or brave. There may, in fact, be a little crying and a temper tantrum involved. The monthly emotional trauma makes me think that I should return to those ultra-frugal days—if only to feel as if I am accomplishing something along monetary lines.

But far more devastating than any monthly expenses is the financial burden of having to purchase every item we own once, twice, and sometimes even three times. I don't know about you, but I can't remember the last time I wore through a pair of jeans. Outgrew them, sure. I can leap over a pants size in one stressful, ice cream-intensive month, no problem. But walk on the hems until I have holes big enough for the heels of my shoes to poke through? Nope. Slide down a hill on my stomach until they are permanently stained and my knees are sticking out? Not in recent memory. Nor, in all my adult years, have I used a pair of blunt-nosed scissors to cut holes in my jeans while they are still on my body. Go figure.

My kids live to do this sort of stuff—which tends to give credence to my "they are trying to drive me crazy on purpose" theory. They break things, write on things, hide them in unfathomable spots. Since they so rarely know the name of the thing ("potato ricer"), they can't tell me where it is, even if their little rabbit brains could remember where they left it. They consume an unbelievable amount of cereal, milk, peanut butter, and granola bars. I mean, you cannot fathom the amount of money we spend on food they eat while they are waiting for me to make them food. Last year I spent more on school supplies than I ever have on an airline ticket.

I'm sure as a mother I'm supposed to find providing for my children more rewarding than perhaps purchasing a round-trip ticket to

Hawaii. Just don't ever ask me to back that up, especially when I'm looking for my potato ricer.

There is a running joke in our family. In every home movie of every child's birthday, my Hubby says the same thing: "Time to get a job!"

Hubby: "How old are you now?"

Child: "Four"

Hubby: "Time to get a job!"

The kids find it hilarious; they think it's just a joke. They don't grasp that it is, in reality, a desperate plea. Seriously, get a job. Contribute. At the very least could you stop spilling peppermint tea on the computer keyboards or cramming cookies in the DVD player?

Our solution, such as it is, is to provide the kids with an allowance, a pathetically small one. Just this side of indentured servitude. It allows us to say, "You have money; buy it yourself," when the little minions start begging, knowing full well there is no way that they have enough cash to purchase the little Polly Pocket hair extension and tattoo parlor that they are salivating over. Brilliant. One less bit of junk around this joint. Keeps the house clean *and* the kids off our backs. Sometimes, I am a genius.

Additionally, we occasionally get all hard-ass on the kids and make them pay for stuff they've broken. (Okay, usually I pocket the cash and use it to buy lattes on the way to work, but they don't know that.) It doesn't take long for the kids to realize that their money supply can dip precariously low in just one particularly destructive episode of "Basement Ninja."

It's interesting to note their various responses to money. Miss Teen Wonder wants money. In fact, she feels entitled to all of *my* money. When we suggest that she spend her own money on a sweatshirt, movie ticket, or class trip, suddenly she doesn't want to go so badly after all. And it's not even that she couldn't pay. I often give her the opportunity to work off a loan, but, nope, she's not interested.

Now, my eldest son is totally different. He is mad as hell that I'm asking him to part with any of his money, but he, at least, is willing to earn it. He's constantly thinking of some way to make a buck. He knocks on doors and offers to rake lawns or shovel snow. He and his friend have attached advertising to their YouTube channel, so they get a fraction of a cent each time someone watches one of their home-produced videos. He would no doubt like me to mention at this point that any grandparent of his who really and truly loves him should be spending a large portion of each day watching and rewatching his movies. (Suggestion: It might be easier just to send him the dollar.)

Given my son's entrepreneurial tendencies, I have great hopes for him. He is also capable of making good decisions as to the value of his purchases. He will not waste his money on crap. If he wants an iPod Touch, he saves up for an iPod Touch. He doesn't lose focus in the middle and go on a SuperTarget spending spree (unlike his momma, who cannot quit that red and white bull's-eye. I LOVE YOU, SUPERTARGET!).

His one downfall might be food. This summer, he and his friends were finally old enough to experience the joy and independence of being bona fide teenagers. I was forced to admit that they are, in fact, responsible and so were given a wide berth to travel sans parents. Thus, every business that sells candy, popcorn, Icees, or French fries within walking distance of our house has begun to reap the benefits of their advancing independence.

That has to be a heady experience, now that I think about it. To have for the first time the ability to choose what and when to eat? Pretty cool. I know that the majority of my teen years were spent socializing wherever food was sold—either food or leg warmers and tuxedo tops, that is. Times have changed, apparently.

I'm not sure how the twins are going to fare when it comes to finances. Taking them shopping is a traumatic experience, and it takes weeks for them to recover. One of the girls in particular is just overwhelmed by the enormity and potential of it all. She runs through the aisles growing ever more frantic. However will she decide? And the thing is, it doesn't matter *what* she chooses, the minute she hands over the cash and settles into the car with her purchase, she is beset with buyer's remorse. She could buy a real live unicorn, adorned with rubies and smelling of strawberries, and the minute we leave the store, she will become silent and pensive and then exclaim, "Dang it! I should've bought the flying monkey."

I've started to encourage them to blow their entire allowance on chewing gum. It's the best way.

Little Man has no money. Ever. Because he loses it—and the wallet it is in—the minute we give it to him. He refuses to leave his money in his drawer. But where does he take it? That, my friends, is the hundred-dollar question. Literally.

We have already talked about Hubby. He doesn't initiate any spending. Well, that's not entirely true. I just ordered myself a new pair of snazzy leggings at my husband's insistence because, apparently, I do not spend enough money on myself. (Is there any doubt why I married him? Other than his near clinical levels of delusion, that is.)

Really, what he meant was that I rarely spend any real money on any one purchase. In addition to absolutely killing at online shopping, I am the queen of the thrift stores and the clearance rack. And yes, many of my treasured finds sport slight imperfections, maybe a wonky zipper or a scuffed toe, but I feel that I can bluff my way through with a certain amount of panache. At least I hope I can—does this outfit look okay to you?

Even if I look like a clown, it's not as if I could quit the thrift shops. I don't do drugs or skydive or shoplift. Currently, the most reckless act I perform is driving our doddering eleven-year-old minivan on the highway. I'm a wild woman, clearly. Without thrift stores, where else could I get the kind of adrenaline high that courses through my body when I've closed in on a magnificent deal?

Example, yesterday I *decimated* one of my local haunts, which was having a sale. Between you and me, they have a deal where they get the leftovers from quite a few high-end local stores, but keep it to yourself, if you know what's good for you.

I scored an amazing, gauzy, pleated tan and mauve skirt that I *know* retails for close to eighty bucks—for $1.49.

I hope to God you put this book down for a minute to applaud. Because that is exactly what you should be doing. That shit is *amazing* and only one of the deals I scored yesterday. I am so good. Really, it's a gift.

The only problem is I have no place to wear my new skirt. In a less positive frame of mind, I sometimes think, what does it matter anyway? Where exactly am I going that I would need to dress up? If I wear anything other than yoga pants and a sweatshirt, I am just being uppity. Absolutely no one would notice if I wore my pajamas all day. This is where Pinterest has ruined me. Just ruined me.

Motherhood is an isolated life, when you get down to it. At first, you are home with the babies, sequestered in a familial fortress of solitude. Everything but the baby is in your peripheral vision, and your scarce interactions with people seem less like actual social events and more like the kind of distracted acquiescence of Grandpa watching football on Thanksgiving. ("Uh-huh . . . Sounds good . . . Uh-huh . . ."). During this phase, I was still sporting those ultra-sexy maternity jeans. What? I had just delivered a baby. I had no time for exercising.

Then the kids get older and more independent, but you still find yourself hustling to get home from work so that they can ignore you from the comfort of their bedrooms. Sure, we're not actively interacting, as the entirety of their brains are taken up with the various little screens they love oh so very much, but I'm sure over the screeching leaking from their earbuds, they can feel my presence. They'd better.

The point is, I rarely go anywhere. Which should mean that I have lots of leisure time, time filled with comfy pants and absolutely no pressure to look good, but, *no*. I had to go and get a Pinterest account. Pinterest is filled with pictures of two-hundred-dollar gray sweaters and designer motorcycle boots, and they are labeled with captions like, "My perfect Saturday outfit" or "casual chic."

When did an oversized Dolce & Gabbana leather purse, which costs more than our last minivan, become the "casual" weekend tote? For my casual weekends, I periodically borrow one of the twin's iCarly backpacks. 'Cause nothing says hip and attractive like Disney off the clearance rack.

So when Hubby suggested that I buy those expensive leggings I'd just drooled over, I jumped on that sucker faster than I would a chocolate cookie. I grabbed the website link for the leggings off my Pinterest board before the words finished coming out of his mouth. Me (totally insincerely) while tapping away on my keyboard: "Are you sure, honey? I mean it's not like I *need* new . . . never mind, I already bought them."

And they are so cute. I cannot regret them at all. Though it has been years since I spent more than eight dollars on a pair of pants and normally the thought of spending full price on anything causes pain to streak through me like kryptonite does to Superman, I love these pants. Maybe it is because I needed a bit of pampering or an antidote to all those stupid, lovely Pinterest outfits, or maybe it is the fact that these are the first guilt-free dollars I've spent in more than a decade.

Family finances are pretty damn terrible. Five kids equals no money, and yet the mortgage company still wants it. Evil bastards. I'm not sure how it works in other families, but I am in charge of all the money in ours. Well, not all the money. Hubby is in charge of our long-term financial planning because he is less apt to either fall asleep or erupt with sudden boredom-induced rage when having to listen to things like compound interest and education IRA benefits.

You see, I'm no good at that side of finances, at all. So Hubby is in charge of the financial planning, and I am in charge of everything else. But that means every time we hit the end of the month and we are *just* skating by, by the skin of our teeth, I feel riddled with guilt. I bought the groceries and the socks and paid the activity fees and purchased the birthday presents. God forgive me if it's December because *it is the blessed birth of the Lord and Christmas requires a certain amount of celebratory spending and I cannot be held responsible for that! Eggnog is not cheap!*

Whew. So, yeah, I have a certain amount of anxiety related to the family's discretionary spending. If only the darn kids wouldn't eat so much or grow out of shoes and jeans and underpants. If only, and here, I wish so much this were true, if only they stopped actively destroying/losing the things we have already purchased—we would have a million dollars.

Okay, maybe not a million, but it would *feel* like a million dollars.

Plus, think of all the time I would save if I didn't have to drive around and replace the missing garlic press, the broken vegetable peeler, the vandalized slipcover. There would be money for movie tickets and restaurant meals and Dolce & Gabbana bags. Well, maybe not the bag, but leggings, for sure.

Except I already have them. SCORE!

Mrs. Jed Clampett

As I've said before, my husband is a sweet man, a good dad, and cute to boot.

He is also a hillbilly.

What brought this to my attention was the long-awaited arrival of Spring or, at the very least, vaguely less winterish weather. When the snow began to recede, it revealed that we had done a horrible job cleaning up the yard before winter hit. Our yard was littered with kids' bikes, gardening supplies, a big ol' bucket, a wheelbarrow, broken trellises, the rain barrel. We were one rusty car carcass away from having a total redneck backyard. I'm sure that my neighbors were thrilled.

Then Hubby made it roughly one thousand times worse. No longer held in check by the unrelenting cool temperatures, Hubby's enthusiasm for gardening was nearing fever pitch, so he decided that he needed some cold frames to properly start his plants. As he was at that moment resting his seedlings on top of my *piano*, I thought this was a brilliant idea. Being the newly converted King of Thrift, however, he did not wish to spend money on this endeavor. He decided to use what we have on hand—otherwise known as "sawing down half the deck railings to use as lumber."

Now the only reason that he thinks he can get away with this scheme is because I hate that ugly deck. I have loathed it since the day we moved in many, many years ago. In his mind, this made it permissible, desirable even. He was using something I didn't even like to make something useful, so how could I possibly be put out?

Here was how I saw it: For years I said, "Baby, that deck is an eyesore. Rabbits live under it. Mosquitoes cluster around it. It is ugly as sin and poorly constructed to boot. Let's get rid of it." And, for all those years, he had ignored me. This year, because he had decided there was something useful in it, he took what he needed, brushed his hands together, and leaving the remaining two-thirds of the deck standing, said, "Done."

Oh, hells to the no, darlin'.

This reminds me of a story. This story is called, "Once Upon a Time, and for No Good Reason, My Husband and His Father Decided to Install a New Showerhead and Tore Down the Inner Wall of My Closet to Get at the Pipes and Never, Not EVER, Put the Wall Back Up. The End."

The same years that I have been forced to endure our dreadful deck I have been living with a tablecloth pinned to the back of my closet. Hubby and his father wouldn't have even finished the shower itself, if left to their own devices. When my mother-in-law and I returned from an afternoon out with a young Miss Teen Wonder, we found the two of them, leaning against the kitchen counter, eating potato chips, and seemingly oblivious to the fact that both the bedroom and the bathroom had been destroyed.

"Are you done?" I inquired, my voice reaching that particularly dangerous octave I magically acquired after marriage.

"Nope." They shrugged. "The pipe is stuck. Nothing we can do."

I took one look at the previously perfectly functional shower torn to bits, the drywall littering my bedroom, and quietly walked upstairs to hyperventilate.

As I was leaving the room, my mother-in-law pointed at her husband. "You. Come here."

A few hours and one shiny, new blow torch later, the showerhead was installed, though we all know what happened with the closet wall.

This shall not be repeated with the deck.

Hubby attempted to appease my wrath by speaking of attractive screen houses with paved floors where the deck now stands and a new patio table. I'd be much less skeptical if he hadn't absconded with my party-time beverage tub and used it to mix cement. The boy has no appreciation of aesthetics, is what I'm saying. Several weeks ago the reception from our outdoor antenna finally got bad enough that we decided we really needed to do something about it. (Other than just break down and pay for cable, I mean.) When I left to get groceries, he and his dad (and you really think I would know better than to leave these two alone by now) were bent over the disc of the antenna, talking about needing a new crimping tool and debating whether or not a new cable was needed.

When I came home, I found that rather than either of those options, they had just duct taped the entire disc to the clothesline post. Not only that, but they expected that I would be thrilled, *thrilled*, that I would now be able to get more than two stations on my television and were genuinely confused when I didn't appear absolutely, deliriously happy. This is why I will never trust Hubby when he says the outfit I have chosen looks fine. He thinks the backyard looks fine. He thinks that monstrosity taped to my clothesline looks fine. The deconstructed deck bothers him not one whit. Now, of course, he also wants to raise chickens in the kids' fort because that is clearly what this slanty, shanty home of ours is missing. The crazy hillbilly.

I'm afraid it's about to get worse. New neighbors have moved in next door. (They purchased their home when the neighborhood was shrouded in a blanket of pristine snow, totally covering our current *Sanford and Son* backyard. The fools.) We noticed the husband out in the yard, checking out the shrubs, sifting through the soil, and setting the boundaries for what we can only assume is a greatly expanded garden.

I realized then that I was about to be replaced. Hubby now spends far more time hanging over the back fence, talking about soil ph with the neighbor than he does with yours truly. And you know what? Good for him. After nineteen years of marriage, I am losing the ability to muster any enthusiasm for topics such as planting zones or germination times. The amount of patience I have for the arguments as to why he needs yet another and better grow light is roughly zero. Our new neighbor, however, loves these conversations. His wife even seems interested, but then, she hasn't been married nearly as long as I have. I use these moments to sneak away to the bedroom and take a catnap, lest I find myself trapped in a conversation with *three* avid gardeners.

There is a trade-off, of course. Without proper supervision, Hubby is free to hatch whatever plans pop into his head. This is a terrible idea. While I was inside, sneaking a siesta, Hubby and the neighbor decided to buy $200 worth of compost. Do you know what another word for compost is? Dirt. My husband paid $200 for dirt. The kids think it is hilarious. They ask me for expensive new sneakers and when I say no, the put on an exaggerated pout, stomp a foot, and say, "Why not? It's only half of what Dad paid—for *dirt*." And then they collapse laughing. I can't say that I blame them. It's as if he came home and announced that he sold our cow for five magic beans, although instead of growing a magic beanstalk, we're just using them to grow regular old beans.

Just for fun, take a wild guess as to how large a two-hundred-dollar pile of dirt is . . .

No. Bigger than that.

Bigger.

Bigger.

Even after both Hubby and the neighbor fertilized all of their gardens, the boulevard, the yard. Even after we pawned off two loads on friends. Even after all of that, it is still roughly the size of a small family of hippos.

"Don't worry," said Hubby, "we have lots of gardeners in the neighborhood. I'm sure they will want to buy some."

They do not. We can't even *give* it away. Surprisingly, "FREE DIRT!" isn't whipping up much demand. So now, in the backyard, with the bikes and the wheelbarrow and the crappy deck and my ruined beverage tub sits a large pile of compost, shrouded in every scrap tarp and errant plastic bag Hubby could find. *Because you wouldn't leave dirt outside, unprotected, obviously.* I think we should just duct tape the antenna to the top of the pile like a crappy cherry on a very, very ugly sundae. Maybe Hubby has done that already. I wouldn't know. I don't go back there anymore. I sit on the front porch and gaze at the yard across the street. That lovely, tidy yard.

Little Hostel on the Prairie

My best friend and her family are coming to visit. I am so excited, except for one thing: they are going to be staying in my house and using my mildewed bathroom and probably looking for a coffee cup in my crappy kitchen. Dang it.

Every time my friend visits, I promise myself that next time, so help me Jesus, I will have done something to improve the state of our home. And as usual, nada. Maybe I should warn her before she gets here: "Remember my house from your last visit? Well, add three years of sticky fingerprints, cat hair, and gouges in the walls. Subtract any repairs that you thought, logically, we would have made by now. And you might want to stock up on hand sanitizer."

I love my friend, and that's why I'm trying to help her manage her expectations. We haven't lived in the same state for decades and who knows? She's probably made some fancy friends. Friends with maids, those little robot vacuum cleaners, or dishwashers.

I'm not going to fare well in comparison.

Today I came home early from work, intent on getting some writing done. I headed to the refrigerator for a drink and found that one of my enterprising children had decided to make cherry Jello. He or she had balanced the large mixing bowl of Jello, with no lid, pre-cariously on a small jar of leftovers on the tip-top shelf. I know that no person alive could have predicted the entire bowl would then topple over, spilling bright red goo everywhere. I mean, what were the chances?

I took in the sight of every single shelf, every jar, every baggie mired in a field of Jello red. "Yup," I thought, "that looks about right."

What is the level of emotional distress right under depression? Despair? Yes, that is what I feel whenever I contemplate someone coming into my house and getting a good, firsthand look at, say, my linen closet or bedroom. My husband thinks I'm too sensitive, but he gets no say in the matter. When I met him, he was living in a single room in a shared house the occupants of which were entirely male. He had a single mattress on the floor, a papasan chair that reeked of cat urine, and no dresser to speak of. I only used his bathroom once, and only then because I was ignorant of the horror that a household of men can enact on a single, shared toilet. From then on, if I had to go, I went—on my bike to the nearest gas station. It was cleaner.

When Hubby and I moved in together, the only things he was allowed to bring were his clothes in a duffel bag, his stereo, and one suitcase, which he promptly shoved into a closet and forgot about. Many months later, while I was cleaning, I attempted to move the suitcase and couldn't believe how heavy it was.

"What the heck is in here?" I asked.

Hubby shrugged.

I opened it to reveal not books, not weights, not a treasure trove of antique coins, but dishes. *Dirty* dishes. Dishes now cocooned with-in a downy, thick blanket of mold. On the day we moved, Hubby had just picked up every filthy dish in his room and, without so much as scraping a plate, tossed the entire mess into the suitcase and brought it to our new home.

This man does not get to have an opinion on home décor.

Aren't I supposed to have a period of time when I am justifiably proud of our home? I had always believed, perhaps foolishly, that somewhere between the era of destructive children and the slow, inevitable descent into my own feral cat- and raccoon-infested Grey Gardens there would be a brief oasis of order and gracious living. Of matching dining room chairs and bathroom towels that did not double as grease rags for bicycle chains. Of reclaimed wooden sofa tables and Jello-free refrigerator shelves. That is the house I want to welcome my friend into, a calm and serene oasis, not the Midwestern version of a highly trafficked, eastern European youth hostel.

"Oh, my goodness," I hear you clucking, "your friends wouldn't judge you. Not if they really love you."

Really? I wouldn't know that kind of nonjudgmental acceptance firsthand because *everybody's house is nicer than mine.* I would love the opportunity to stroll into a friend's house, take in a water-damaged living room wall or a gaping and structurally suspect hole in the floor, and be able to assure them, and myself, that what makes a home special are the people who live within its walls not the *House Beautiful* tableau it presents. I'm not sure what it would be like to see a person's home and feel compassion, instead of envy. I imagine I would feel a little bit like Mother Teresa.

In any case, it's too late now. I'll clean before they get here (you know, any area they might actually see, which means not behind the sofa or in the laundry room. Let's not get crazy here.) and then I'll engage in the kind of visual slight of hand that I always do—pull out the "good shower curtain," the one with fewer mildew stains and cut a boatload of flowers, and put them in every room. I'll grab a few citrus candles, so at least the place will smell clean. And nobody, but nobody, is allowed to make Jello.

What's a Mom Gotta Do to Get Some Respect Around Here?

At some point, my two eldest children decided it was open season on their mother. In the past, I have been grateful for the close bond they enjoy, but now that one of their shared interests is mocking me, I'm rethinking my opinion. Lately, when the three of us are together, it isn't long before one or both of them is parroting me—in a voice that clearly sounds *nothing* like me. *They* find the act hugely funny. I, on the other hand, couldn't be less amused.

Here is a partial list of things they use for ammunition:

1. My veganism. Much like my religious beliefs, I hold veganism to be a personal and private decision. Despite having some decidedly opinionated views on the subject, I know that no one wants to hear them, so I tend to keep them to myself. I really don't want to become the evangelical, snake-handling, doomsday prophet of dinner. However, those two knuckleheads perceive my hesitancy as weakness, which is why they light into me about it every chance they get. This past Thanksgiving, Hubby and I had our heads together,

painstakingly planning a menu (that included, I will have you know, *a turkey*—because I am awesome and inclusive, god-dammit) at which point my son sauntered in, listened for a bit, and said, "You know what I'd really like? *If everything were vegan.* Also, let's not eat too much. And maybe go for a run." For one shining moment I thought I had been making head-way with one of the young'uns, but no. Apparently all they've learned from me is sarcasm.

2. My absolute fear of what plastic is doing to our health and the planet. That stuff is everywhere and in everything. While I try to be discreet about my dietary beliefs, when it comes to the sheer bulk and adverse effects of all that junk, I resemble a crazed Chicken Little, flailing my arms in the air, yelling that the sky is falling. Our water is being poisoned, I cry, and so are our bodies. My daughter thinks I am insane. Her imita-tion of me consists of running in tight, little circles, waving her hands at her face, and yelling, "TOXINS! OOOOOOh the toxins!" Listen, kid, I don't want my grandbabies to be born with two heads. Is that so wrong?

3. My music. Hey, it is not my fault that music peaked back in the '80s with the Smiths. It was good then, and it is still good now. Of course, they disagree. What is patently unfair about the whole thing is that they don't like when I listen to cur-rent music either. Which I do, for the record, because I find certain songs inherently danceable and not because I am "at-tempting lame hipster coolness." That leads to number four.

4. My dancing.

And, yes, I did recently attempt to make my own lip stain out of beets and vodka, but sometimes you just have to try things—for *science*. Like when I learned that you could make cake from just a cake mix and a can of soda. It's true. Cake mixes were originally intended to be a "just add water" convenience product, but folks wouldn't buy them because it felt too much like cheating. So the cake mix manufacturers added the bit about the eggs and oil. Sales shot through the roof. Crazy, America! Escape the tyranny of eggs and oil! All your cake mix needs is a can of diet coke or a mug of coffee. You're welcome.

I'm not even sure what the lesson is supposed to be here and who is supposed to be teaching whom. Is it don't take yourself too seriously? Never show weakness? Or maybe it's to stop picking on your mother and show some respect, you ingrates, or she will pack up her bags, move to Arizona, and leave you alone *with your father.*

I probably shouldn't even let the teasing bother me since it comes from love, or at least that's what I'm telling myeslf. I only notice it for two reasons: the nonstop nature of the ribbing and the fact that I recently read a self-helpy type of book that cautioned about stooping to self-deprecating humor. According to the book, if you make fun of yourself, you are basically attempting to convince the world not to take you seriously. That you are, in short, a buffoon. At the time, I scoffed. But now I'm not so sure. (Note to my children: I am a serious, grown-ass lady, thank you very much.) Yes, I poke fun at myself, but given that the majority of my comedy revolves around the subject of mutant chin hair, which is clearly not my fault, I don't feel that I am devaluing anything worthwhile about my inherent self or capabilities.

Also, let's talk for a moment about our fragile, human egos. I have what is probably common in first-born children—an extreme fear of making mistakes. An erroneous move on my part invariably leaves me sweating and short of breath.

Joking about myself isn't flagellating myself for being an inept shell of a person; it is reframing the entire event as something so light-hearted that, if it had happened to anyone else, would only have proved how utterly adorable we are in our fallibilities. I am a forty-six-year-old, graying, middle-aged woman with five kids who all suffer from selective hearing and you-are-not-the-boss-of-me-itis. I have a husband who plots yearly to sneak chickens into our backyard, and I toil daily in the soul-crushingly ugliest kitchen in the world. Occasionally I am called to chase raccoons out of their nest in my house. Don't make fun of myself? How is that possible?

What my children don't understand is that they could learn from me in those moments. It's my job to show them that publicly admitting one's mistakes is not that big a deal. Several of my kids have such extreme responses to even the thought of making a misstep that they make me look positively nonchalant about the whole thing. Recently, I received an email from one of my children's teachers. This child, who shall remain nameless, had been engaging in some pretty typical talking in class, yada, yada, sort of stuff. Nothing serious, but still, nothing you could responsibly ignore. When confronted, this nameless waif went, and I say this with love, apeshit. There was crying, bitter accusations, name-calling, attempts at emotional manipulation, and above all, the absolute insistence of innocence. The hysterical child refused to concede for one second that there might have been the teensiest justification for the teacher's email. We both agreed a cool-off time in the bedroom was needed.

After awhile, I grabbed a bag of jelly beans and crawled into bed with the juvenile offender. I doled out a handful of candy for each of us and said, "You know, when I make a mistake, I'm so embarrassed. I think that everyone can see how stupid I am. I'm pretty sure no one is going to like me because now they know that I'm a phony and, underneath it all, a big dope." We both stared at the ceiling and quietly ate our jelly beans. "But the thing is," I continued, "that has never, ever happened. My friends still love me. My family loves me—at least I hope you all do—and I screw up every day, *all the time.*"

Can I just recommend jelly bean therapy to each and every parent out there? We laid there for a few minutes, munching away, and then I heard a sigh and a little voice, "Okay, Mom. You might be right. Maybe there is a chance I was talking in class . . ." The voice went on for a while, although I lost the thread of the conversation for a few minutes, light-headed as I was from hearing the words "Mom" and "you were right" together in the same sentence. In the end, we had a lovely talk about how our behavior sometimes gets away from us and how we could, maybe, stop that from happening in the future. But the truly important lesson is that we don't have to be afraid of looking at our mistakes. We all make them, and it doesn't make us terrible or stupid or unlovable. If anything, we are endearing and hilarious—at least, that's what my two eldest kids tell me.

The Reason I Am Not a Motivational Speaker

Today is Sunday, the one day of the week that Hubby and I are both home from work. Obviously, it is my favorite day because of Hubby, of course. Mostly. But also because we get to sleep in and—due to the fact that both of us are technophobic to the point of achieving honorary Amish status—read an actual newspaper.

We were doing just that on this fine Sunday when we heard a commotion in the yard. The tire on one of the twins' new bike, which we had purchased a mere six days previously and which she had ridden a grand total of maybe eighteen minutes, had exploded, for no discernible reason.

Of course, she absolutely needed to use the bike the next day to get to and from her summer program, which is why we bought the darn thing in the first place. So now, instead of a nice, leisurely afternoon with absolutely nothing but free time (I do not sully my Sundays with housework), we faced an afternoon of schlepping the bike back to the store and attempting to convince the service desk people that really, goddammit, the thing exploded all by itself. They aren't going to believe us. I sure as heck wouldn't.

At the thought of the task ahead of us, Hubby's face went a little gray, and he looked about ten seconds away from shaking his fist at the uncaring God in the sky. "We were done with that," he said weakly, "*done.*"

I gave him a consoling hug, the simple, naive dope. "Oh, honey," I said, "we'll be done when we're dead."

It's true. My life is a series of moments of déjà vu. I can't tell you how many times I have found myself folding a pair of jeans or standing in line at the store or picking something off the floor and thought, "Wait a minute, didn't I just do this? Didn't I just wash this? Didn't I just buy one of these, like, yesterday?" I swear I wouldn't complain as much if I were toiling away at some new task because that at least would feel like my life had some forward momentum. Instead, I feel like poor Sisyphus, cursed by the gods to roll a slippery stone up a mountain for all eternity—only my stone is made of dirty socks and unsigned permission slips.

The unrelenting demands on our time didn't used to bother my husband at all. He used to have a borderline psychotic belief in our ability to fit in just one more thing.

"No," I would say, over and over, "not unless that thing is strangling you with these actual hands."

I remember a summer, not long ago, when we were, as always, flush with children but not cash. At the time, I had to get home from work by five forty-five because I was driving our one vehicle and the evenings were scheduled to the hilt. One child needed to be at t-ball at six and one needed to be at baseball at seven fifteen, presumably after everyone had been fed. My teenage daughter was pleading with me to take her to get a haircut because the next day was her birthday and for some reason we had established the tradition of a yearly birthday makeover. I had presents to wrap, muffins to bake, a house to decorate, in addition to the normal laundry/cleaning/housework type work. In the midst of everything, I called my husband and asked him to please walk down to the park and pick up our youngest (whom had been deposited at t-ball) because it was starting to rain at which point Hubby mentioned that he needed the car because he had an (attendance optional) union meeting. So, I did the only logical thing; I hung up on him.

Flash forward to the next day. I was at work attempting to get all our orders done pronto so that I could leave early and be home when the birthday girl got off the bus. I wanted to make her favorite meal before it was time to bundle her and her best friend off to softball and take our twin daughters to t-ball. That's when my husband decided to call and inform me that he was considering *picking up a weekend job*. Because apparently, though I was losing my mind from the craziness of our schedule, we actually had oodles and oodles of extra time, though I couldn't imagine where it would be.

We had one car, two full-time jobs, five kids in softball five nights a week, and *three* kids with games on Saturdays, Mondays, Wednesdays, and the occasional Sunday. My darling, deluded husband had volunteer committee meetings. Additionally, we had weekly drum lessons, vision therapy, not to mention the *couples therapy* that we were clearly on the verge of requiring.

"I will beat you senseless," I said. "I will beat you and then divorce you and I will *not* take the children with me."

"Ha, ha," he chuckled, "We'll talk about it when you get home."

I should have got in the car and made a break for it. Dummy that I am, I went home.

We're still busy, just about every minute, it feels like. My one consolation is that now Hubby feels the stress, too. I think it might be because I now work each and every Saturday, leaving the weekend errand running to him. I almost feel a little guilty about it, to tell you the truth. On Saturdays I get up, put on my nice clothes, and meet my good friend and coworker for coffee before we spend the day working, yes, but in a fairly controlled and leisurely way. Hubby gets up, runs kids to baseball games and voice lessons, scurries from one errand to the next, shops for groceries—like I said, I *almost* feel guilty. I pretty much just handed the poor man his own rock.

I hope our schedule is the reason for his harried look because, otherwise, the only possible explanation is he has begun taking on my stress via our decades of association, like a contact allergy. Am I the irritant he has been exposed to for far too long? You always hope your partner brings out the best in you, right? That they encourage you to develop strengths you didn't know you had. But I suspect it works the other way, too.

Hubby has traditionally been a cheerful sort. He's a morning person, who springs from bed assured that good things are going to happen. I, on the other hand, am a wee bit more subdued. He has a tendency to stroll about the yard, singing to himself. I am more inclined to hang questionable slogans on the walls that don't so much inspire me as hopefully postpone my eventual need for mental health counseling or anger management classes. The latest reads: "We do not have the luxury of despair." I hung it where I can see it when I wake in the morning. It's meant to convince me to get up, already. Stop procrastinating. I have too much to do, too many people counting on me. I do not have the luxury to lie in bed, sighing, like Camille. What I *do* have is the justification for a mild case of alcoholism.

Yesterday, Hubby attempted to describe an unfamiliar feeling he had been wrestling with.

"I feel, I dunno', not good," he began. "Anxious. Not that anything is going wrong, but that something bad might happen."

"Dread?" I suggested.

"That's it! I am feeling a vague sense of dread."

Oh, crap. It was totally me. All that fretting—years of sleeping next to me while I laid awake pondering the financial ruination that could possibly befall us or worried about the terrible lives our kids might lead if they don't take school seriously, learn to hold their tongue, or tell time on an analog clock—had seeped into his slumbering brain and turned his formerly optimistic self into, well, me.

Maybe it's not too late to be a better influence. I bet I could cheer him up about this whole exploding bike tire fiasco. "It'll be done in no time," I could tell him. Or, "Boy, you take such good care of your kids." Still, you have to admit that my original statement has a certain ring to it: "We'll be done when we're dead." It's punchy; it's concise; it's vaguely inspirational.

Yup, that sucker's going on the wall.

Running Away from My Problems

should tell you all about one of the great loves of my life. Nope, not Hubby or the kids. Surprising everyone that has ever known me, I started running about eight years ago and fell in love, though you couldn't exactly call it love at first sight.

The whole thing started under duress. Okay, that's not entirely true. No one actually physically forced me to start running. What happened was that my husband decided to run the Twin Cities Marathon.

"But I don't wanna run a marathon," I whined.

"You don't have to. I'm going to do it, though," he countered.

"Why? Why do I have to run a marathon?"

"You don't."

But I did. Stubbornness, pride, and what I like to think is a healthy competitive streak mandated that if *he* was running a marathon, by God, I was running a marathon. I was thirty-eight, had never exercised with anything approaching enthusiasm, and—did I mention?— I was fifty pounds overweight at the time. What could go wrong?

I'd love to tell you that training was an epiphany, that angels sang and I discovered a hidden talent and a joy inherent in physical exercise. But I didn't. I was and remain genetically talentless when it comes to running. I complained mightily as we trained, swore when the temperatures rose over that never-ending summer, and nearly struck Hubby every time he suggested adding a few extra blocks to our long training runs.

We finished that year with two seconds to spare, the sweeps bus literally an arm's length behind. Given the Universe's wicked sense of humor, it was hardly surprising that I had a much better experience than my husband. He was plagued with cramps and stomach problems, while I was high-fiving the crowds and choosing to forgo Gatorade in favor of the beer and champagne offered by spectators at makeshift rest stops.

Gatorade is for chumps.

Somehow I kept running. Since then, I have run multiple half-marathons, marathons, and trail runs. I agonize over my snail-like pace, kill it on the hills, and litter my Pinterest boards with images of funny race tanks and colorful running shoes. Hubby sometimes will run with me, but more often, not. Running never really struck a chord with him, which I guess is another of the Universe's little jokes. He's more likely to act as my support crew, pedaling his bike beside me, carrying my water bottles and packs of energy gels, and offering words of encouragement when I get tired. Encouragement that sometimes ends in me muttering obscenities more or less under my breath. Luckily, he is a forgiving sort. This year I am going to attempt a fifty-mile ultra-marathon, and something tells me I'm going to need that support crew. Or a medic.

For one Mother's Day, I asked only that we run a 5k together, as a family. Training was difficult for my eldest son. He ran, stony-faced and resentful. When I attempted to offer a few, well-meaning tips, he hurled his water bottle into the bushes and yelled, "Can we *please* not talk about running *while we're running?*"

Hubby barely stifled his laughter as he no doubt experienced a strong sense of déjà vu. What can I say? Like mother, like son. I count the fact that my son has become a dedicated member of his school's cross-country and track teams as one of the greatest victories in my life.

Right now I am at the start of another training season. I'm supposed to be losing weight in preparation, but I am doing a miserable job of it. In the never-ending up-and-down pendulum of my stupid weight, I am up to the very razor's edge of my last pair of fat pants. My fattest pants. I don't know why "all my underwear are too tight" is not considered a legitimate reason to skip work, but it should be.

So, clearly, I am not running for the weight-loss benefits. I wish to God that worked for me, but it just doesn't. I have never lost more than two pounds during any racing season. Weight loss for me happens in the off season, when I am free to lie listlessly on my couch as my caloric intake lessens, lamenting both the loss of my vibrant energy and the will to live. The remainder of the year, I attempt to comfort myself with the thought that should I ever be picked for one of those *Survivor*-type reality shows, I will be able to live off my accumulated paunch for months. Plus, I'm super-fit, which nobody would see coming.

I'm also not getting an anti-aging boost from my running either. I just had what was, in retrospect, an unjustifiably malicious interaction with a woman at work. She was in our shop, buying a present for her grandniece, and we got into a discussion about our families. I mentioned that my first born had just entered "kindergarten."

"Did I just say kindergarten?" I said, correcting myself. "I meant college."

"I was going to say!" she responded, far too enthusiastically for my taste. "I thought, 'Whoa, did she get a late start.' But then I figured I misunderstood and you were probably talking about your granddaughter."

See? That right there is the kind of statement that justifies my inherent distrust of strangers.

So, no weight lost, no shared interest with Hubby, no fountain of youth—why am I doing this again?

I'll tell you why: because all my life I have been plagued by anxiety.

A restlessness that lives clenched around my stomach or snaking between my shoulder blades. I have, at various times, tried to hold it at bay using positive thinking, meditation, or journaling. Mostly, I try to sedate it with chocolate in all its various forms. (Never underestimate the power of chocolate. Also, liquor.) But none of these methods, none, has had the calming effect of running. I love it, especially when I have been extra twitchy. When I feel like a hamster, caught by the tyranny of the wheel, I just run and run and run until I feel calm and strangely rested. Clear, like water. Even just thinking about it calms me down.

And now that I am contemplating an ultra, I am seeing another benefit. How often do we get to say that we are "all in"? How many of us really lay everything out there? I'd love to say that I am all in when it comes to my kids, but I'm embarrassed by the number of times I've managed to sneak away and watch a movie or disengage in some similar way. We live in a land of comforts that makes it too easy to distract ourselves with our texts and our Netflix and our cat videos. When I think of the upcoming challenge of running fifty miles, what I'm drawn to is the feeling of being completely engaged in a task, used up. I want to cross the finish line and know I couldn't take one more step, that I am utterly done.

Except we aren't, right? The truth is, in a few minutes or a few hours, we'll be up, walking around, kneading our sore muscles, and irritably scrounging for cake. Or maybe that's just me. The miracle of running is that we finally know, no matter how much we have done, there is more just under the surface. We learn that we are so much more, that our limits are much larger than we ever dreamt—unless I perish of a heart attack right on the spot, and even then, who knows?

Running, more than exercising my body, works on my wishy-washy optimism. Underneath all the doubts and fears (I'm not sure I can do this; I'm so slow; I look like a manatee in spandex) is the slowly blossoming idea that I am a fierce and immutable force of nature. That my success is inevitable, as long as I never stop moving, no matter how slowly that happens to be. What a gift, if I can manage to get it into my thick skull.

Today, I was hit with the kind of situation that tends to send me into a hand-wringing frenzy of anxiety. The absolutely awesome news is that the nineteen-year-old biological brother of our three youngest kids found us on Facebook. Clearly, he is much smarter than we are, as we had been attempting to do the exact thing but were stymied by spelling discrepancies. Since he tracked us down, we have been exchanging messages whenever our two time zones allow it and slowly getting to know each other. Though we haven't spoken with their biological mother or grandmother directly, it is a great comfort that we can relay the details of the kids' days back and forth via the magic of the Internet. Today he sent me the message that I have been expecting: He wanted to know what our future plans were for him. He wanted to know if he could move here, live with us, and join his siblings.

I feel so ill-equipped for this situation. I'm too worried about everyone in this scenario to be at all effective. When I think about this young man, I think about him as a young boy, losing first his father then his little siblings. The thought that he ever felt abandoned or alone makes me want to tell him to come to us immediately. Then I think about his mother, the sudden deaths of her husband and her father and the resulting hardships that sent her three beautiful children to us—are we really going to encourage her remaining son to leave? Understand that I am always desperately wanting to do the right thing. I just really wish that in this situation someone would tell me what the hell that is.

I was practically paralyzed by my uncertainty and doubt but simultaneously vibrating with nervous energy. I only knew one way to get rid of it, so out the door I went for a run.

"Calm down," I told myself, "stop worrying. All you are responsible for right now is this run." But even that bit of advice, I realized, was a tall order. I needed to focus on one single moment at a time. Suddenly, a great calm rushed into my body. I ran like this for a while, refusing to look ahead even ten minutes. "Just this step. This one. This one." It was maybe the easiest run I've had in my entire life.

Lately, I've been so nervous about my ultra-marathon goal. If you could see me, you would know that nothing about me screams "extreme athlete." You would never think, "Right. Her. Clearly participating in an ultra-marathon." A Netflix marathon, maybe. That's how I see myself as well. Thinking of this challenge has given me nightmares and actual, physical hysterical hives. But today, for about the first time in my life, I managed to calm down and focus on the present, and I could see why. I get ahead of myself, always. I'm not running fifty miles tomorrow; I'm running it in five months. A huge part of the stress in my life is the uncertainty of knowing how to get from here to whatever is out there. I mean, seriously, I just want to know. I see the end goal of any of life's challenges, and between me and there is a dark chasm of unknowing.

It really bums me out.

I am not afraid of hard work; I just would like a clear road map, please. A thousand times people have pointed out that this is not good for me. "Enjoy the journey," they say, and to my credit, I have never struck them. There are many of us for whom the journey is traumatic and fraught with danger, nothing but dark hallways that lead nowhere and mazes with trapdoors. Given the lack of a current road map, I feel the need to imagine all possible scenarios for all possible paths and before long find myself feeling overwhelmed, as if all of them are happening at once.

Today, for whatever reason, it was easier to set those thoughts aside and just focus on the few feet of path directly ahead of me. It really didn't matter how far I'd already come, or how far I had left to go. There was just this step and the next one.

I returned home, much calmer and clear-headed, determined not to run ahead of myself. The kids' brother does not need for us to orchestrate a permanent move from his home in Ethiopia to here *today*. I do not need to jump into the vortex of citizenship and college transfers and work visas and Homeland Security *today*. Perhaps we could start with a visit. A simple family visit. A single step toward a journey we're starting on together. Though he won't be with us, physically, when I attempt my fifty-mile trail run, he will have made a huge contribution to what I hope will be my eventual success. Our fledgling relationship reminds me that, while the finish line is wonderful, it is all about the run. So keep your head up, wear cute shoes, and don't forget to thank your support crew.

Happy trails and good running.

Karma

I am currently, absolutely, wretchedly sick. It serves me right.

For the past several years, I have been in perfect health, free of both illness and accident, a fortunate circumstance I credited loudly and often to Hubby as a testament to my superior constitution. You would think that I, who knows better than to tempt fate, would keep my crowing to myself. But I did not. Inevitably, the tide started to turn.

At the beginning of the winter, I decided to prepare myself for the next year of running by engaging in the recommended activity of "cross training"—an activity I have avoided (along with stretching or weight training) for the entire eight years of my running history. I just like to run. Period. I do not like being strapped to a machine and flailing about, going nowhere. I do not like hoisting metal bars upwards and down, up and down. It reminds me too much of an afternoon I spent at a local home for delinquent boys (when I was far too young to appreciate the possibilities. Ah, opportunities missed.). I was friends with the daughter of the House Mother, and she invited me over to play. From the living room window, I could see two boys, moving concrete blocks from one side of a field to the other. When they were finished, they turned around and stacked them all on their original spots. (Naughty boys, caught smoking—or so I was told. Even then, I had hoped their transgression was a bit more scandalous than that.) This went on all afternoon.

Now, whenever I attempt to motivate myself to start a new fitness routine, I see those boys pointlessly trudging back and forth, back and forth, which is probably why I so rarely force myself into the gym.

Still, I am getting older and thought it would do me good to take a break from running, so once again, I started at the gym, riding the bike, swooshing on the elliptical machine, and tackling the stair climber, whereupon I immediately tore a calf muscle.

Fabulous.

Still, I could lift weights, and since I planned on doing much more trail running, I decided to embark on a general strength training plan of my own design, since I am, obviously, an expert in all things. This led, not surprisingly, to me irritating an old rotator cuff injury to the point that I couldn't heft a coffee mug without wincing.

A week later, I was working in the kitchen, a chore I have found is more pleasurable when streaming comedies on my iPad. I was giggling away, chop, chop, chopping at the cutting board when I put a little too much attention on the show and not enough on the exact location of my chef's knife.

Chop!

I felt that sucker go right through my nail and immediately went all woozy. I stuck my head around the corner and gave Hubby a wide-eyed look.

"Um, help?"

He was furious. He hates blood and cuts and medical emergencies of all sorts. Still, he was helpful and supportive, as much as one can be from another room entirely.

"Sit down on the couch!" he yelled from the safety of the dining room. "Put your hands over your head! Besso, press down on the towel! Sam, get some ice!"

"Not sure I need ice," I protested.

"SAM! ICE!" he bellowed, glowering at me from afar. "What were you doing? *Why* weren't you more careful?"

In the end, he *did* instruct the kids to bring me a glass of wine, so that was useful. And I learned a few things, too. For example:

1. First Aid kits are absolutely no good if no one knows where they are.

2. Neither are they much help if they are soaking wet from being stored in the car under a leaky back window.

3. Do not think, "Oh, thank goodness it is only the middle finger of my left hand. I hardly use that at all." This is false. This is an extremely useful "helper" digit and necessary for a host of activities. Removing your contacts, typing, and communicating with fellow drivers all come to mind.

4. Facial cleansing pads are not "just as good" as a sterile cotton bandage.

5. Watching *Ab Fab* from across the room while attempting to chiffonade basil with your very best knife is probably, in retrospect, not a good idea.

6. Really, there are few things funnier than trying to show Hubby your scabby, nailless finger. I can't recommend it highly enough.

Because I am my father's daughter, I never went to get the stitches I clearly needed. ("Who needs doctors?" was our family motto. Once, my dad broke a tooth and I saw him Super Glue it back together.) I waited out the three days it took for the blood to stop flowing by piling on ever more bandages and describing my fledgling scab in minute detail to my husband. Good times.

Now, on top of torn muscles and cut fingers, I have a cold. I was up all night, sneezing, eyes and nose running, coughing up what seemed to be bits of soccer ball, and sweating buckets. I felt like I was being dissolved from the inside out, like a foil-wrapped Easter bunny left too long in the sun. The only thing that cheered me up was the thought that clearly this illness would have killed a lesser woman.

Karma is a bitch, ya'll. That's a lesson straight from my childhood, though then we credited it to God smiting you for your uppity ways. Me walking around, bragging that I was impervious to germs and injury, well, I'm lucky I didn't wind up with malaria or brain fever. It's not that I believe that the Universe is evil or tricky, but I do think it's apt to make you work for your blessings. That being the case, I tend to keep my head down.

I have many friends who would suggest that this attitude is the reason for many of the stalls or ills in my life. The Universe (according to them) is awash with treasures, yours for the asking. And I believe it, too—for them. Let me be clear; I think that the Universe has been ridiculously generous with me. Sign me up with all the "#blessed" girls out there, posting pictures of their little babies, a sunset, or the perfect latte. It is good to appreciate the little things and remember to be thankful. I think I'm pretty darn good at it. Asking for more seems, to me, downright risky, like enjoying a good run on the nickel slots in Vegas and then deciding to try one's luck at the high-rollers' table. Half an hour later you've lost your house, your savings, and doomed your children to a lifetime of serving watered down gin and tonics to the patrons of some casino—and not a good casino on the strip, either. A seedy one, near the airport.

This inherent lack of faith might be holding me back. Hubby thinks so. The other night we had a lovely date. After an amazing concert, we enjoyed leisurely drinks and a prolonged discussion about what, exactly, is wrong with me. What? You don't do that? Sure, it sounds like the kind of experience that one would relay to, say, a divorce attorney as justification for an exceedingly generous alimony settlement, but I assure you it is much more caring than it sounds. I was thinking, in fact, how lucky I am to have a partner whom I believe so wholeheartedly is in my corner, that when he suggests that I may be acting in a way that runs counter to my interests, I can listen to his criticism without indulging in hysterics or, say, homicide.

I didn't always feel that way. I remember once, much earlier in our relationship, when he suggested, gently, that I had talked too much at a party. Mature person that I was, I burst out in tears and was resentful for weeks. "I'm going to call my mother," I'd announce loudly, "unless you think that would be *talking too much*." Still, twenty years of unflagging support, coupled with the seriously annoying habit of being right more often than not, has earned Hubby the privilege of stating his opinion without fear of bodily harm or emotional retaliation.

Hubby's stated theory was that I could, perhaps, accomplish more if I let people help me. I have tremendously loyal friends, he pointed out, all of whom would be willing to support me in a hundred different ways if I wasn't so hell-bent on convincing them that I am fine, thanks, everything is under control.

"Dude," I responded, "I'm from Wisconsin. The only things people are allowed to give me are casseroles and seven-layer bars. And usually someone has to die for that to happen."

For those of you not from the Midwest, we are a people who take great pride in our self-reliance. We do things our own damn selves, and the thought of accepting or admitting that we need help is fraught with danger, causing us to act, most often, like traffic cops at the scene of an accident—move along, folks, nothing to see here.

We are the people who drive ourselves to the emergency room, rather than ask our friends across the street for a ride, and we only go there in the first place if the wound is heinous enough that we see actual bone. (Honestly, I don't know why Hubby is so smug in his assessment of my inability to seek help—especially since our eldest daughter once said of him, "Dad wouldn't go to the doctor if he were growing a *tail*.") I know it isn't just me because I have oodles of friends with exactly the same affliction. All of us march along, insisting that we do everything ourselves.

Let me tell you a joke:

One spring a terrible flood hit a small town. The water rose so quickly that a man found himself trapped on his roof, unable to get to safety.

"Please save me, Lord," he prayed, then settled in to wait.

A short while later, a neighbor floated by on a raft.

"Get in!' his neighbor encouraged.

"No, I'm fine," the man insisted, "the Lord will save me."

A while later, a speed boat came by.

"Get in!" the pilot said. "The water is still rising."

"I'm fine," the man said again. "The Lord will save me."

A while later, a helicopter hovered over the house.

"Climb up!" yelled the pilot.

"The Lord will save me," he insisted and stayed on the roof.

He drown.

When he got to heaven, he marched right up to the Lord and demanded, "Why didn't you save me?"

"What do you want from me?" God said. "I sent a raft, a speed boat, and a helicopter."

It is possible to change. I have met numerous folks who have managed to set aside their insistence on muscling through alone. They are open and receptive to help, wherever it may come from and in whatever form it takes. They are remarkable, as seen through my eyes. Happy, relaxed, and, dammit, effective at getting what they want. One of them happens to be my son.

My eldest son is a little magical, I swear. He manages to bring things to pass that his mother believes are impossible. His long-term goal is to work in movies, and so he got it into his head that he wanted to speak to a working director. Did he sit in his room, ruminating over how on God's earth he could possibly make that happen? Nope. He spoke about it, often and to people who maybe knew someone that could help. Before you could say, "Lights, camera, action," he had been introduced to a local director, who not only spoke to him and his friend about what a director does but let them work on his movie. The director invited them to peer through the camera at his framed shots and explained why he made the choices he made. He even let them work as extras in the film. SammyJ leapt at every opportunity that was presented him and ended up with an abundance of experience and his own credit in the film. The show-off.

So there is a slight chance that I may be wrong. That depending solely on oneself isn't a sign of strength, but an indication of the limits we impose on ourselves. If there is any sort of karmic lesson here, it may be that in learning to accept the help and support offered to us, we also open ourselves to learning how to give. Alone, we are the little Dutch boy, attempting to hold back the tide, stuck in place, with our fingers in the dike. Together, we could erect a new wall, divert the stream, or move the town. Which makes me thing that maybe karma isn't a bitch after all. Maybe karma is a speed boat or a helicopter, or a neighbor who offers to watch your kids when you are under the weather, or a husband who has your best interests at heart.

Always Look on the Bright Side

In advance of my father-in-law's visit this past weekend, I had to spend a great deal of my precious time cleaning our house.

Cleaning is no bueno.

Our house required a top-to-bottom scrubbing, especially since Miss Teen Wonder had been living in the basement family room for the entirety of "J-Term" because, yes, we had given away her room roughly thirty seconds after she left for college. (Sorry, chica, but when you move, you lose.)

Anyhoo, I was chugging along, tidying the bits and pieces of daily life that had been flung, willy-nilly, throughout the place, vacuuming, *dusting* (for the love of Pete), when I inescapably found myself mired in the thankless, soul-crushing task of cleaning the bathroom. Seventeen years ago, flush with a completely unfounded confidence in our untested ability to renovate our new home, Hubby and I attempted to replace the tile surrounding the shower. It was a horrible, horrible error. We did not have the money, tools, or knowledge to complete the job competently. As a result, the motif of our bathroom has become "Black Mildew" or, possibly, "The Bitter Tears of Regret."

Cleaning the shower is a weekly exercise in self-flagellation, which is, in its own way, useful. As one brought up in the Midwest, I learned early on that the worst trait a person could have is an overblown ego. God forbid we become "braggy." No worries of that around here. Should I ever suffer a spike in self-confidence or personal satisfaction, all I need to do is take a shower. One look at the state of the caulk around the tub and I will be reminded of my criminal lack of home maintenance skills— to say nothing of the irresponsible parenting involved in allowing five children to live in a house clearly riddled with toxic mold.

On the upside, my math skills have improved vastly due to my frequent calculations as to the declining resale value of our home.

I can only hope that our houseguests are kind enough to extend us clemency, based on our good intentions. The kids clearly have. Whenever they hear Hubby and me talking about our desire to sell this place in favor of an itty-bitty alley house the very second our youngest leaves for college, they become outraged. To them, our house is friendly and cozy—just the sort of place anyone would want, black mildew notwithstanding. They probably don't even notice the caulk, which is just about all I can see every time I enter that room. What I wouldn't give for a pair of magical blinders that would allow me to gloss over the many things that annoy me. I'd wear them in the shower, in traffic, at the gym, in the morning when I have to interact with children before coffee, and definitely when getting weighed in the doctor's office. (So unfair. Who gets weighed in the middle of the day, after lunch, wearing shoes, or God forbid, snow boots? Is it any wonder that sometimes my subsequent blood pressure reading is through the roof?)

I realize that one of the goals of spiritual or emotional growth is training myself to see the good—not the mildew—all around me. It shouldn't be that difficult. After all, here I am, a healthy woman possessing virtually all the creature comforts one could desire. I am tapping out my ridiculous complaints on a tablet that has far more computing power than the first Moon rover, but, nevertheless seems far too slow, especially when I am trying to watch *Sister Wives* over on Netflix, dammit. Black mildew? Get over it, Danke.

I think it's a case of getting my cause and effect all mixed up. My line of thinking is thus: If my home is perfect, lovely, and magazine photo shoot ready, clearly all the interactions within it will be, too. A beautiful environment will spawn naught but warm, mature, and caring words from the people who live within it. I imagine that if my bathroom were lovely (as well as the kitchen, living room . . .), life would be seamless, calm, and quiet. The children would play harmoniously on immaculate white couches, dinner times would be rife with engaging and (quietly) raucous conversations, and we would probably take up putting puzzles together as a family. You would see us through our front windows, a golden light surrounding our perfect tableau, all members around the table, our heads bent low as we murmur words of encouragement to each other.

Right.

It works the same way when I consider my weight. I'm certain that if I lost ten (fine, twenty) pounds, I would be successful in all things. My self-acceptance and confidence would grow exponentially. If I lost twenty (thirty) pounds, I would love myself every minute of the day and take exceptional care of my body. This book would be finished; my health would be exemplary; my teeth would be whiter, my hair somehow shinier. I would be happy, confident, energetic, and successful, if only I lost thirty (thirty-five) pounds. It is so much easier for me to believe that the only things stopping me from living a life so perfect that it is usually only seen during holiday crescent roll commercials are a messy house with ragtag furniture and an unhealthy devotion to peanut butter toast and brownies.

Here's the truth: White slipcovers and an unstained living room rug do not generate a warm and loving family life. Because I'm an adult, it really shouldn't matter how many pairs of muddy shoes are strewn in the entryway or how many dirty plates litter the counter or how rarely the cat box gets cleaned. Being an adult is being responsible for my feelings, for my pouty, "It's not fair!" way of thinking. But it is hard, hard, hard. What encourages a warm and loving family life is me being, you know, warm and loving.

Isn't that the pits?

Maybe it wouldn't be as difficult for someone who isn't a first child. Who isn't wound rather tight and, since we are being honest here, doesn't love to compensate for her own slovenly ways by attempting to exert ultimate control over her little fiefdom.

I have found, though, that the quest for perfection gets easier when you are too tired to chase it. Frankly, these kids have worn me out, which has led to the sort of backsliding that doesn't improve the general cleanliness of our home but does wonders for my blood pressure. Also, I've jettisoned some things that seemed important to me at one time, but now I have neither the time nor force of will to worry about anymore. For example: When Miss Teen Wonder was but a babe, I was committed to her intellectual development. I painstakingly constructed high-contrast flashcards of complex geometric shapes to tape to the backseat of our car for her to gaze at while strapped backwards in her car seat. The idea was that, with constant stimulation, her little brain would develop its maximum capacity for math and other intellectual pursuits. Flash forward several children—Little Man wanders in looking for help sounding out a word in a book and I, dumbfounded, demand, "Who taught you to read?"

Answer: nobody. Have enough kids and the little buggers just pick that all up via osmosis, I guess. My point is *not* to ignore your kids and let them grow up to be ignorant knuckleheads, but maybe just don't worry so much about it. They all have inherent skills and gifts that you actually have little influence over. At least that's what I'm telling myself.

So I've given up worrying. Bam. Cold turkey.

Okay, I'm trying.

Right here, in the front of my brain, I believe that, yes, this is a mostly benevolent universe; that most people mean you no harm; that when hard times hit, it is possible to find a soft place to fall, be it into the comforting arms of family and friends or your own hidden well of strength; that you can grab hold of misfortune and shake some sort of blessing out of it.

Snaking around the base of my skull, however, is that nagging, persistent sense of doubt and anxiety. I am keenly aware that when

I open my eyes in the morning, I, like everyone else, have no firm guarantee of what the day will hold. I hate that.

The better, more optimistic me thinks, "It could be great. The weather's beautiful, the kids are well, maybe you'll get something good in the mail." (I don't know why I think somebody might have sent me a present virtually every day of my life. It used to be disappointing until I discovered online shopping and cut out the middleman. Who can find a better present to get me than me?)

Sadly, most days I can't even hear that voice. If the kids are healthy, I'm worrying about their grades. I worry about the pooch of fat that sticks out over my misnamed "skinny" jeans. I worry about the decreasing gas mileage of our minivan, the financial health of our household, and my genetic tendency to hoard magazines and reusable food containers.

Nothing in there remotely declares that Life is GOOD! And it is. It's a freaking miracle every minute.

It's worry that is keeping me from my highest good, not my alleged character defects that I constantly fret about such as my love of diet sodas. (Although given the studies on the potential detrimental health effects of artificial sweeteners, I may meet my maker a lot sooner if I don't give up the stuff. But I can't worry about that right now.)

All that worrying stands in the way of simply enjoying the world around you which would be a particular shame right now. We've entered the most glorious time of the year here in Minnesota. Finally, after twenty-eight months of winter—a conservative estimate, if you've lived here at all—it is spring.

Ah, the precious milestones of the new season: the first night's slumber with open windows, the season's inaugural gin and tonic, the happy wiggling of newly bared toes, the first evening your husband makes a mad dash through the living room, slamming shut windows, because your harpy-like screaming is echoing, clear as a bell, down the block.

Despite my best intentions, last night Little Man worked my absolute last nerve. My tantrum was awe-inspiring in the sheer breadth of vocal theatrics; there was my high-pitched, ear-piercing shriek of "What could you possibly be thinking?" flush up against the deadly calm and dangerous baritone directive, "Don't you *dare* interrupt me." It was a performance worthy of Laurence Olivier's Hamlet, though now that I think about it, it was probably closer to Jack Nicholson in *The Shining*.

Thing is, I am not the least bit apologetic about my outburst. (Don't judge. You don't know, people. You just Do. Not. Know.) In my experience, sometimes you need to yell to drown out the voice that is telling you to go into the kitchen and start smashing plates. The thing that chaps my hide about the whole situation is that it came hot on the heels of a new resolution of mine, one that goes hand in hand with leaving worry behind.

It occurred to me, that while I have an endless list of goals, both immediate and far-reaching, I have never set a goal for myself to simply be happy. Being happy is always desirable, of course, but I've always seen it as an elusive by-product of another event—not the carrot I strive for. I've been pondering how different my daily decisions would be if my guiding criterion were "Will this make me happy?"

I immediately thought of scores of things I wouldn't be doing or would do quite differently if I paused long enough to consider this question. It seemed revolutionary and vaguely blasphemous, given my "pushpushpush!" approach to most things. Right there I decided, I was going to set my intentions to be happy first and foremost and worry about everything else, well, never.

Then my stalwart intentions were bested by an extremely stubborn child and all hell broke loose.

I've been thinking and thinking about what I could have done differently that would have allowed me to fulfill my parenting obligations and simultaneously maintain my equilibrium. The problem as it stands is this: I think parents are the bearers of authority in the home and should be respected as such; Little Man thinks I should go soak my head. Honestly, whenever you find yourself yelling, "Yes, I *am too* the boss of you!" at a child, you have lost, my friend.

How do we change this situation? Clearly, he isn't going to bend. Pleading, "Mommy wants to be happy, so please stop being a colossal pill" isn't going to do much by way of changing his mind. Which means changing this sticky dynamic is going to come down, once again, to me. And that's getting old.

I'm going to have to decide that some things just aren't worth the fight. Some things are, but maybe I could let go of being so personally affronted by his misbehavior. Maybe. It's going to take a lot of practice. Fortunately, I don't think that'll be a problem—he's young, after all. I'll probably get to practice being calm and unruffled three or four or twelve times before supper this evening. Besides which, if I ever manage to achieve utter perfection when it comes to parenting, I'll still have the black mildew in the bathroom to encourage my ongoing personal growth.

Heigh Ho, Heigh Ho, It's Off to Sleep I Go

Are there any people over the age of thirty who aren't exhausted all the damn time? They must exist, right? I probably just don't see them because they are out and about, frequenting places called "bars" and "movie houses" and "sit-down restaurants." I have even heard that some of them voluntarily leave their house after seven at *night*. I have a vague memory of doing this myself, so I can only assume this "nightlife" still occurs but the thought of dragging myself out the door at the end of a long day? Inconceivable.

This is the general mind-set of most the folks I hang with. ("Hang" being defined as "Facebooking each other with hilariously worded, but nonetheless whiney, complaints about our day.") I recently did a major sweep of my closet, vowing to rid myself of anything I do not wear on a regular basis. It was depressing to see how many truly lovely, sparkly dresses I own that have never even made it out of the bedroom. When, exactly, would I have need of a black, netted and sequined formal frock? And these lovely vintage heels over here? Yes, those—the ones covered in dust.

Ugh, heels. The very thought makes me wince. Even my feet are tired.

A while back, I purchased a Groupon for a local natural foods restaurant. I'd had that sucker for nearly a year before Hubby and I gathered ourselves together enough to venture out on a beautiful weekend afternoon. When I placed our order and presented the coupon, the cashier apologetically rejected it, explaining that it was only good for dinner.

She might have as well have given my money back right then and there. I couldn't imagine when that was going to happen. It took us eleven months to shore up the energy for *lunch*. The only way I could possibly appear for dinner is if you gave me a bendy straw so I could consume my soup with my head flat on the table. I can barely manage supper at our house. Because of Hubby's work schedules and mine, dinner time happens late in our home and the sole reason I don't consume my supper lying on the couch is because I am trying to set a good example, dammit. I will admit, however, that I have completely stopped nagging the kids to slow down when they eat. "Eat *up*, children," I say now. "While it's still hot. Go, go, go!"

This deep-seated fatigue is playing havoc with my productivity. When I am tired, anything that isn't absolutely essential goes right out the window. "Essential" activities pretty much translate to "keeping the coffee pot filled and not letting the offspring be eaten by wolves." Other than that, you are on your own.

The women in my family—and by that I mean my sister, Miss Teen Wonder, and myself—are notorious for our hedonistic love of shuteye. Well, that's not quite true. What we're really known for is being absolute ogres in the morning, a talent in which my daughter has managed to surpass even me. Many is the morning that the six conscious members of our family have stood at the foot of the stairs and argued in urgent, hushed tones about who would be taking their lives in their hands and attempting to wake my eldest daughter.

Seriously, the girl is scary.

On the upside, her aim is terrible, since her eyes are screwed tightly shut against the searing pain of a single ray of light. I find the best way to approach her is to blind her with a direct beam from her desk lamp, and while she flails blindly, shake her once, forcibly, while yelling ironically, "Good *morning*, sunshine!"

Yeah. I'm gonna pay for that someday.

Not that I'm much better. I never want to wake up. I get up because I have to get up. Because there is always something that I didn't quite finish the day before. Because the people in my house like to eat food and wear clean clothes and that darn maid never shows up (perhaps because she's imaginary). And I never, not once in the past twenty years or so, have opened my eyes and thought anything other than, "Oh (sigh) crap."

When my eldest son was young, he used to burst into our bedroom at the first, distant glimmer of sun, throw open our curtains, and in a wee voice trembling with the excitement of untold possibilities warble, "Get up! Get *up!* It's morning time!" The excitement of it all was almost too much for him to bear, and as I remember it now, it almost seemed as if he clutched his little chest as he spoke, overcome with emotion. To him, a new day signaled a new magical adventure—and why not? Food mysteriously appeared before him when he was hungry, he had no responsibilities, and unanticipated gifts would occasionally appear for no discernible reason. Adoring adults laughed in delight at nearly every verbal pearl that fell from his lips, so, yeah, I guess I'd be excited to get up, too, if all that was waiting for me.

No, that's a lie. My mother assures me that I've always had a love affair with sleep. When I was young and misbehaving, my mom used to send me to take a nap which she says wasn't punishment at all since I so happily complied. It got me out of her hair, though, so it was clearly a win-win situation.

Part of the problem is that I can't make myself go to bed at night. Even though I love few things better than to stretch out in bed, I can't seem to tear myself off the couch. Now that the kids are older, they don't go to bed themselves until late, which means just that many more hours of chaos. Nighttime is the only peaceful time in our home. And there is just something about a quiet house that I cling to.

Every other waking moment of the day a child is talking to me, no, scratch that, talking *at* me. I do not move without being followed by an endless stream of words—I swear, so many words that they actually achieve a physical density. To accomplish anything—preparing a meal, paying the bills, a trip to the bathroom—I have to wade through a barrage of words, sticky as mud.

So, when they finally stop, how can I be expected to plop into bed? Though I mostly fritter away my time on celebrity gossip sites, bad television, or usually both simultaneously, there are plenty of nights I just sit on my couch and stare, shell shocked, into the air.

I have even tried setting the vibrating alarm on my activity armband to 9:00 p.m. in an effort to encourage me to shut off the computer and start getting ready for bed. Between you and me, it isn't going well. Until that alarm can shake my arm forcibly enough that I drop whatever bit of electronic distraction I am holding at that moment, I don't hold out much hope of its success. What tends to happen is it serves as a reminder to change the next morning's alarm from my well-intentioned six o'clock wake-up time—which would allow me to get something accomplished before work—to seven thirty, at which point I have just enough time to stare resentfully over my coffee mug for twenty minutes before running around like a lunatic, ever more conscious that I am, goddamnit, going to be late, again.

I can't blame my perpetual morning scramble entirely on lack of sleep. I have to admit that the other half of the problem is a decided lack of enthusiasm about my day. My daily rundown of everything I have to do—get kids to school, work out, do the laundry, wash the dishes, work, repeat—engenders depression more than eagerness. I'm trying to change my attitude, but it's *hard*.

Our neighbor describes it as being "in the tunnel." Work, kids, work, kids—head down and nose to the grindstone. It's true, though we all know that it's only part of the story. (At this point, my conscience and, perhaps my children's future therapist, demand that I mention that motherhood is dearly important to me. Yes, I love them, and clearly, their little faces should be reason enough to bound joyously out of bed. But their little faces come attached to just so much work.)

Obviously, we parents wouldn't raise children if we didn't value them so highly. I mean, seriously, how much easier would it just be to toss the little buggers out the door and take a nap? Don't answer that. It might make me cry just a little bit. I think the answer is that I need to add more fun into my daily routine. Something to look forward to other than coffee, or liquor, or, um, wait, what else?

Right, the children. Yes, I meant to say: first the children and *then* coffee and *then* liquor. But something else would be nice, too. Something that required nothing of me other than to show up and enjoy the experience. Like a weekly massage or a regular happy hour meet-up with my girlfriends (oops, that's liquor again).

I know that people say hard work is supposed to be its own reward. (And by "people," I mean my father.) But sometimes, hard work is just that. Hard, stupid work. Sometimes, when you haven't had the opportunity to recharge and regroup, you start to overlook the little moments that make it all worthwhile and that remind you why you are working so hard in the first place. Face it, if you spend too long with the nose to the grindstone, it becomes difficult to see anything other than that spinning rock. When that happens, no amount of sleep is going to make you greet "morning time" with anything other than sullen distrust. Believe me, I know.

So I think that it is in the best interest of all involved if I resolve right now to find those things that will make me feel optimistic, revitalized, and energized. It may be hard, having to pamper myself into a more positive mood, but I think that it's best for everyone if I start now. I'll do it for dear Hubby; I'll do it for you, my darling friends . . .

I'll do it for the children.

Memories

Sometime, just for fun, ask your kids what they remember about growing up. You will probably be surprised to find that their recollections of your family's shared past are very different than your own. I say this because recently Miss Teen Wonder told us how we, her adorable family, were winning her new friends via her vivid descriptions of our shenanigans. I had no idea what she was talking about, as I consider us pretty darn normal. Sure, maybe we're a little louder, more chaotic, and prone to minor, mostly unintentional vandalism, but by and large normal. Right?

To our daughter's new friends at college, apparently not. For one thing, many of them are only children. So any of the antics one might get up to with four other little people who are simultaneously your fast friends and sworn enemies is downright fascinating. The thought of having a little brother is endlessly entertaining, even more so when you can throw in tales of chasing him around the yard until his too-large, hand-me-down sweatpants fell to his ankles or stories of dressing him in a floor-length skirt, accented with purse, earrings, and daring red lipstick then introducing him to the neighbors as "Rosita."

The poor little brother.

My money-pinching ways are also good for a giggle. I would just like to point out that I'm sure that there are plenty of other intelligent and kind children who, in lieu of sufficient funds for formal summer camp programs, would have loved Camp Danke. Camp Danke happened in our home, and opening day occurred bright and early the second week of summer vacation whereupon a highly detailed and, if I may say, exceedingly attractive schedule appeared taped to the wall of the kitchen. Brightly colored blocks of time filled a poster board, all heralding the fun, fun, fun (!) activities we would be engaging in for the next several months. Activities such as:

Library time! (Mondays and Fridays, 10–11:30)

Beach picnic! (Tuesdays, Wednesdays, Thursdays 12–3)

Music madness! (piano practice, daily half hour in the afternoon, rotating schedule)

Global cuisine! (Thursday evenings)

Newsletter production! (Wednesday mornings 10-11)

Country of the Week cultural studies! (Tuesdays and Thursdays 10-11)

As you can see, it was amazing fun—just look at all the exclamation points! Oh, sure, my kids may roll their eyes at the memory but show me any other summer camp that allowed you to study the Amharic language via the Ethiopian equivalent of *Sesame Street* videos and also taught you how to make curried cream cheese wontons. There are none, I tell you. *None.*

Also, there probably aren't many other families who, when deciding that the mortgage payment was probably more important than the annual trip to the state fair, went so far as to recreate the experience in their backyard. I spent a week fashioning a giant pig out of a refrigerator box, making carnival games, and tracking down cotton candy and official State Fair Corndogs in the supermarket. And did it win my children's undying love and devotion? It did not. It did, however, bring Miss Teen Wonder and her new friends closer together in their shared laughter over the cardboard pig, so that's something.

Rotten kids, they only remember what went wrong. Like when our goal of swimming in all of the Great Lakes during a single vacation forced us to take our final dip in a particularly fetid bit of Lake Erie.

"Watch out for dead fish and abandoned needles, and whatever you do, *don't open your mouth!*" I yelled. To this day, I am surprised our vacation souvenirs didn't include at least one bout of hepatitis.

To be fair, the kids' assessments of our family vacations aren't wrong. They are often terrible. There was the spring vacation we decided to take my mom to Lambeau Field, mecca for any Packer fan, and we ended up inching across the state in a blizzard that dumped seventeen inches of snow on our stupid, stubborn asses. Again, I stress that this was our *spring* vacation.

Or there was the year that we made the rounds of all the grandparents and assorted family only to discover at the last stop—in my in-laws' meticulous downtown Chicago loft—that the three youngest kids had been sharing not just batting helmets with their t-ball team, but head lice as well. (Which is probably, actually worse than all the holiday vacations we arrived spreading joy, cheer, and also the flu. We are, not undeservedly, known as the Typhoid Mary of the extended family.)

And lest we forget, there was the time we exploded a bird.

Before I tell you about it, in my defense I would like to state that I try really hard to plan for these vacations. I consider everyone's needs and interests and try to anticipate various situations that might arise—to the point that pioneers probably didn't pack as much junk in their covered wagons as I habitually cram into the minivan, you know, just in case.

Hubby is zero help. With five kids, he has never thought to pack so much as a diaper. He wakes up on the morning of the trip, grabs whatever is handy, pulls on a pair of pants from the floor, and starts bellowing that it is *"Time to go."* Never mind that some of us are

packing for six and have been doing laundry for three days in antici-
pation. We have driven straight across this country more than once,
and to his mind, the only true travel necessity is a bag of beef jerky.

'Cause, you know, kids *love* jerky.

On the bird trip, Hubby didn't come at all, so I was free to bring
whatever I thought we could possibly need. We had books on tape,
Frisbees, softball mitts and balls, jump ropes, snacks, bottled water,
medicine for just about any ailment up to and including food poi-
soning—none of which helped us when the bird hit the windshield
at seventy miles an hour and every last wet bit of avian debris was
sucked into the car to ricochet off various screaming individuals until
we could find an exit ramp.

We spilled out the doors, shrieking and laughing hysterically. The
twins were convinced that they got the worst of it, since the body
of the deceased bounced off their legs and landed at their feet. But I
claim that distinction for myself, emerging from the car, as I did, hair
and clothes dripping. Bird guts in your hair pretty much trumps dead
bird at feet.

Now tell me, what could I have packed for that?

The hero of the day turned out to be Little Man. While the rest
of us were still shouting "Eww!" and running around the van rubbing
ourselves with hand sanitizer, he calmly got a plastic bag, found a
tent stake from our last vacation, and scooped up all the bird bits.
For the rest of the car ride, whenever there was any disagreement
between the kidlets, Little Man got *exactly* what he wanted, which
pretty much ensures he will be telling this story to his friends until
the end of time.

Nothing I do right or well can compete with these memories. I've
pulled off hundreds of perfectly lovely dinner parties, orchestrated
thousands of harmonious family evenings and probably a few whole
vacations where nothing went wrong but those memories are yawn-
ers. Nobody wants to talk about them. To be perfectly honest, these
things that happen to us, well, they could happen to anyone. It's just
that, for whatever reason, they happen to us so very often.

Like the time we brought home a cat from the humane society

that turned out to have both a chronic bladder infection and fleas. When my eldest son told me he had found the dang pests on the cat, I promptly *freaked*. You are maybe thinking, "What's the big deal, Lanie?" But that is because you didn't live through the Great Batting Helmet Lice Infestation of '06. And that's what fleas are—cat lice. They get in your bedding, they get in your couch and your rugs, and they are not selective biters, either.

So I headed into Petco thinking I should probably just burn the house down and start from scratch, but the nice, reassuring sales lady seemed to think that was a bit extreme and suggested that with a little quick, decisive action on my part, I could nip the whole thing in the bud. (You gotta love a store that purveys both pet food and psychological counseling.)

So I spent the afternoon medicating the cat, washing everything that fit into the machine, and dousing everything else with flea napalm. And yes, I am aware that walking across, sitting on, and breathing in pesticides seems to some a whole lot worse than dealing with bugs but to that I say, "Bugs! Eww!"

But by far our daughter's favorite story is about the summer we spent attempting to evict a family of raccoon squatters from our roof.

It didn't go well.

My sister called it immediately when I complained to her about the aggressiveness of our furry trespasser.

"Baby raccoons," she stated.

"No way." I said. "This raccoon is just stubborn."

Then I went back to my somewhat unscientific attempts to make life as unpleasant as possible for our unwanted tenant—bug bombing it and whomping it on the side of the dormer with a shovel, yelling, "Go away, you stupid raccoon!"

It was even less effective than you might imagine.

Eventually, the raccoon took to standing on our back steps, claiming dominance over the yard. This was a problem since we were in the midst of having our front steps redone. The raccoon's backyard occupation meant we had to resort to entering our home by grabbing the edge of the front door's frame and hoisting ourselves four feet into the house. The kids thought it was a hoot. I, with the natural grace of a drunken elephant, found it an inelegant solution at best. So we called in a professional.

"Baby raccoons," he said. (From across the state, I felt a strong psychic "I told you so" from my sister.) He then proceeded to tell us there were signs that, in addition to the dominant mother and her offspring, we had been housing whole legions of raccoons over the winter and more than likely had been for years. Also, every raccoon ever born in the house is now imprinted with its location, putting our home on its short list of desirable housing.

I had a sudden urge to buy a bigger shovel.

When I looked sufficiently woozy with dread, the exterminator laid out the plan: More than any predator, momma raccoons fear male raccoons. Apparently the males will rip little baby raccoons apart. (Let me tell you, this put a lot of things in perspective for me. I mean, Hubby and I sometimes disagree about how to discipline the kids, but at least he doesn't dismember them.) Our guy, upon locating the female's entry point, proposed smearing the opening with something he called "Boar Juice." Momma raccoon, when she went out to forage, would get this stuff all over her fur and carry the scent back into the den. Sensing a threat, she would pack up shop and move her and the babies out of there.

What is Boar Juice? Well, that would be the blenderized innards and sexual organs of a male raccoon, of course.

Double eww.

I'm trying hard not to think about the karmic ramifications of that. I mean, it can't be good, right? I try to be kind to all creatures. I don't consume any animal products a solid 98 percent of the time. My largess, however, does not extend to raccoons. After I mulled the plan over, I have to say that I began to appreciate the, um, sincerity of the gesture—painting my house with the blood of my enemy, as it were. I felt a little like Michael Corleone in *The Godfather*: "You come into *my* house? My house? "

The more I thought about it, the more I liked it, so I gave our guy the go-ahead.

We had been holding our breath, waiting for the raccoons to leave for about a week when—surprise!—we had bats in the house. Because, of course, we would. The girls clambered down the stairs screaming and yelling for Hubby to get the bat out of their room. Watching them, as best as I could from behind my mostly closed bedroom door, was like watching a Benny Hill rerun. A mere minute after the bat was ushered outside and the girls returned to their room, we heard Miss Teen Wonder let out a shriek.

"The *raccoon*! The *raccoon*!"

And there she was, Mama Raccoon, standing on her hind legs and peering through the girl's dormer windows. I swear the animal narrowed her eyes and pointed right at me.

Oh, crap. I wasn't dealing with a raccoon; I was dealing with the *devil*.

What I wish the kids would remember is that we eventually triumphed and rid ourselves of our furry pests. But success is fleeting and those memories don't seem to stick. Like it or not, our mishaps are the stories they hold dear: the visiting lice, the putrid swims, the demonic raccoons. They relay the story of me attempting to chase away the raccoons with a shovel so often that I'm convinced they will work it into the eulogy at my funeral. But since I'm pretty sure they will be laughing, I guess they are good memories after all.

Home Sweet Ramshackle Home

For weeks, we have been living with a bucket under our kitchen sink, which has sprung a leak, and not a little one, either. We had already acclimated ourselves to using just one sink, since the other had started leaking months ago. We were happily pursuing our normal fix-it routine—which is to occasionally sigh heavily and stare pointedly at the offending appliance or fixture, trying to guilt the other spouse into action. Unfortunately, the loss of not one but both of our sinks had robbed us of the ability to wait each other out, preferably until we move into a nursing home. Then it's the kids' problem.

This repair promised to be a colossal pain in the behind. Our house is creeping up on one hundred years old, which means it is full of both charm and nonstandard (and sometimes potentially fatal) features. One time we hired an electrician to try to make some sense out of our crazy electrical system. Setting aside that all the "off" switches were actually "on" switches and vice versa, one of the main problems was that the entire first floor, with the exception of one outlet, was wired to a single fuse. This meant that if someone were to, say, turn on the microwave in the kitchen and another person attempted to vacuum the living room or dry her hair in the bathroom or any combination of the above, the entire first floor lost power.

This happened a lot.

Blessedly, our electrician was able to separate out the wiring for various rooms as any normal, sensible person would have done in the first place. Not to talk smack about the previous owners of our house, but I feel confident in asserting that all their home improvement projects were undertaken with a hammer in one hand and a vodka and NyQuil cocktail in the other. And although I thought that the first floor was our biggest problem, it turned out that the upstairs bathroom actually posed a greater challenge.

I was working with the electrician, helping him figure out which room was wired to which unmarked fuse. My job was to turn on the lights in the room and stand there while he pulled fuses, then yell when the light finally went out. I was standing in the bathroom, watching the lights burn and thinking that, really, this was taking a ridiculously long time, when the electrician came to the foot of the stairs and asked why I wasn't telling him when the lights went out.

"I will," I said.

"But you didn't," he insisted.

"But I will," I repeated.

"But you didn't," he intoned.

I was thinking that he might have been enjoying a little cocktail action himself, when he stomped up the stairs and then stopped short, shaking his head disbelievingly at the sight of the bathroom lights, blazing merrily away.

"Son of a bitch," he said.

Frustrated with what he thought was my inattentive assistance, he had worked his way through all the fuses and finally cut power to the entire house—and the lights were still on.

To this day, I have no idea how he managed to fix that without electrocuting himself in the process. Which is why I was so skeptical when Hubby crawled out from under the kitchen sink, brushed his hands together briskly, and said, "Easy peasy. The pipe has corroded away. Five dollar fix, one hour tops."

Five dollars, he said.

One hour, he said.

Of course, first we needed to go to the hardware store for pipe, then return to the hardware store for a proper wrench, which turned out to be too small. One more trip to the hardware store. One more wrench. Plus two additional sink stoppers because, what the heck, both of ours were broken.

Now we had the proper wrench, but the pipe was stuck, frozen to the trap.

Hubby had me look up solutions in our handy fix-it book.

"It says to tap the trap gently with a wrench," I said.

My husband, still naively cheerful, says, "Okee doke!" And—tap—still stuck. Tap. A little more forcefully—Tap! Tap! Taptaptap-taptap TAPTAPTAP TAP!

"Let me try," I offered, gave the sink one heartfelt TAP, looked at Hubby, and shrugged. "I've got nothin'."

In the end, we had to replace the pipe, the traps, and the entire sink. The sink was of a size that, of course, is no longer made, so we had to enlarge the hole with a jig saw, which we broke. So Hubby used his Sawzall®, which tore a huge chunk out of the laminate top of the counter. At this point, it was eleven o'clock at night, so I smeared some calk around the piece and slapped it back on the counter, figuring the sink will hold it in place. Except the sink didn't fit. Hoping to spare his delicate sensibilities, I told my husband to avert his eyes and hammered away on the back lip of the sink until the damn thing fit in the hole. Success.

The only thing left was to connect the pipes. This was the point at which we discovered that we were short four inches of pipe. You would have thought we were staging our own production of *Macbeth*, what with the wailing and gnashing of teeth and rending of garments, but no. Typical home improvement project at our house. Several days later, I was able to make it to the hardware store for the missing length of pipe, which I connected and which, of course, still leaks.

Hubby is sure we can fix it, no problem, but I'm leaving it there until we retire and move. Really, we've got at most twenty-five, thirty years, left in the house. I can live with that. I think, for the sake of my sanity, I'm going to have to learn to. Otherwise, it's just too frustrating.

For years, I have placed myself under a great deal of stress about darn near everything—my messy kids, my messy life, and my house that is slowly falling in around my ears, one broken appliance and permanent marker spree at a time.

Often times this free-floating dissatisfaction will congregate around the subject of my ugly, repair-resistant little home. This morning, in the midst of a near anxiety attack over the sorry state of the carpet, it struck me; I just plain don't have the capacity to pull it off. It is an oddly comforting thought. Why is my house not beautiful? Because I am inherently incapable of producing and maintaining that perfect *Home Beautiful* tableau. I am not failing through lack of will; I don't have a chance to succeed because my DNA precludes any sort of success.

This is a positive realization. Maybe first children *do* tend to think that the sun revolves around us, but I am here to tell you, that is not always a good thing because we tend to shoulder the blame for all the imperfections we perceive in our environment. We also believe that if we just strive a little more, clearly we could make everything the fuzzy, peach-colored vision of bliss that we imagine. To even consider the possibility that falling flat on my face is, in fact, inevitable? Holy smokes! I can't tell you the pressure that relieves from the top of my skull. I'm actually feeling a bit giddy.

And were I just to accept the fact that my home is never going to be the epitome of design, I probably wouldn't be so paralyzed by the utter helplessness of it all. Many are the moments that I sit, overwhelmed and unable to perform even one home improvement task because, short of tearing the whole place down and starting from scratch, nothing is going to help. Our home is where old couches go to die, where utility reigns over beauty, and where the color motif is "stain."

At some point this past year, I just gave up. I don't have the money to combat the decay, and I certainly lack the energy. But now, I don't know, achieving a certain amount of pragmatic acceptance has made me happy to do what I can.

One of the words I've always loved is "tidy." "Tidy" is different than "clean." "Clean" has a certain antiseptic remoteness, but "tidy" conjures up images of industriousness and careful attention. A thing can be well-worn and still look loved. (As a person speeding mightily toward middle age, let me just say, I certainly hope so.) That seems to me a more achievable goal. Sure, our sideboard is scratched and beat-up, and has been since the day I scavenged it from the side of the road, but when I take the time to polish it, I begin to value the service it provides. Same when I rearrange the cupboards or scrape the jammy fingerprints from the fridge. Somehow just the attention I bring to my home through these small actions makes a difference. And shouldn't I do it, anyway, just to respect the small fiefdom where our little family lives? To honor the place where we all live together, for what is, after all, a terribly short amount of time. Our home provides more than protection from the weather, more than a storage area for school papers, snow boots, and Mommy's box wine. It gives us a sheltering arm in which we come together to live and laugh and fight and grow. The beauty of my home is in the faces of the people who live within it.

A new sofa wouldn't hurt, though.

Rejection

One of the twins has grown into the stereotypical sullen teen girl. The idiotic utterances of her family are met with eye rolls and the deep sighs of the heavily afflicted. She keeps a running narrative under her breath about the injustices being done to her and should you question her perceptions or, indeed attempt to engage her in a companionable conversation, she will spin around and briefly affix you with a narrowed-eye glare of such intensity that I often find myself taking a backward step and clutching for my pearls. Well, I would, if I wore them.

Do not mistakenly think that this is behavior she exhibits to the world at large. Au contraire. Outside of our home, she is a sunny, friendly person. I have seen her curl into my mother like a cat, content to be cuddled and petted for the better part of an afternoon. She is helpful and sweet to her classmates and neighbors. I periodically receive glowing and unsolicited emails from her teachers, congratulating me on the fine job I am doing, raising such a sweet, funny, kind, and sociable girl. If I were a more honest person, I would be forced to admit that I'm not sure how much influence I could possibly be exerting on her since her daily routine is to drop her school things in the entryway and make a beeline for her room, where she vanishes for the better part of the evening.

"Fine," I dream of yelling outside her door, "I didn't want to talk to you *anyway*." But I don't because she may come out and harm me. Okay, she wouldn't really do that, at least I don't think she would. (And please don't tell her that I said she might. You know, just in case.) But it is difficult to avoid taking this rejection personally. I mean, I am a lovely person. Just lovely. I have much knowledge of many things that might be useful to a young, inexperienced person such as my daughter and she doesn't want to hear any of them. *None* of my kids do, now that I think about it. And I'm not just talking about those random bits of knowledge that progress has rendered obsolete such as how to fix a cassette tape or work the kinks out of a phone cord. The only thing my kids hope to learn from me is the password to their parents' ATM card.

When they choose not to follow my sage advice on the little things, it's annoying, but now that my kids are growing into their own, watching them stumble through some truly heartbreaking situations is excruciating. Whoever decided that kids need to learn these lessons on their own? Preposterous. They are babies; they literally do not know anything. Yet, they are genetically programmed to believe that somehow they possess more knowledge and ability than their brilliant mother.

Like I said, preposterous.

I should be used to a life of rejection. Back in the day, I would have bet money that a music producer would have seen my sweet, sweet moves and plucked me, Courteney Cox-style, from the rest of the Doc Marten-shod and red lipstick-wearing crowd, ideally to star in a Pearl Jam video.

Nope.

Later, I had dreams that my amateur pottery attempts would lead to bigger fame. Perhaps my professors would see great potential in my interpretation of form and take me under their wings. But, alas, I remained undiscovered. My one claim to notoriety was one of those "person on the street" interviews. Sadly, when the article appeared, my comments were credited to one "Melody Dodge" much to the amusement of my friends. Oh, and once, I won an *Onion* magazine "Caption this photo" contest.

It's a good thing my inherent sense of self-worth isn't based on worldly recognition. I'd be so sad I wouldn't be able to raise my head off the pillow most mornings. Which is why it is important to be able to muster those accolades for your own self. For example, I know myself to be an excellent cook, comments from my children notwithstanding. I am also an excellent dresser, or would be, if I could afford any of the outfits I drool over. I have really good, thick hair, and if I ever did more than cut it myself with a sewing shears, there is a good chance it would be even better. Also, I have a certain flair for time management as evidenced by the realization several years ago that there is no conceivable reason to fold underwear or socks. Bam! Literally hundreds of hours saved over the course of a lifetime.

In addition, I have matured to embrace an admirable lack of vanity. Like, right now, I am sitting in a coffee house, and it has occurred to me that I have absolutely no idea what I look like. In the whirlwind of activity this morning, I actually never looked in a mirror, not even to put on my lipstick. I might be sitting here, looking as haphazard as Heath Ledger as the Joker, and does it even bother me? Actually, now that I think about it, yes. Yes it does. But I'm eating oatmeal instead of a slab of coffeecake, so I should get credit for that, at least.

Wouldn't it be fun to get together with your girlfriends and have a party celebrating those accomplishments that tend to go unnoticed? Let everyone make themselves sashes and giant glitter-covered "Winner" ribbons. Maybe take turns crowning each other "Best Thrifter" or "100% On Time with Birthday Cards" or "Most Patient in the Face of Malfunctioning Technology." We all try so hard to get through each day with some level of confidence, good humor, and grace, which earns us no credit at all. And it should.

History is littered with persons who wrote spectacular novels or spawned social movements or advanced their particular field but were utter jackasses to the people unfortunate enough to love them.

Neglectful parents. Unfaithful husbands and wives. Unfeeling children. They get applauded by history, while those who move less spectacularly but so much more kindly through their lives are rarely thanked for the deep contribution they make in all our days. I would much rather spend time with a funny and compassionate barista than a brilliant and insufferable theorist any day. And yes, all those contributions to medicine and literature improve our lives, but so does a respectful interaction with a stranger or a smile from your best friend.

The problem with tying our self-worth to those big, splashy promotions at work or other public acknowledgments of success is that we forget that the most important work we often do happens in the quiet moments of the day, unnoticed by nearly everyone. It's nice to be of service to a cause, but are we being of service to the people we love? To the people we share our particular corner of the world with? To teenage girls who don't even want our help in the first place? Far too often, in my case, the answer is "no." But I keep trying to get better at it because, in the end, that is the measure of success that is important to me.

It is disappointing to me that, if I were to be totally objective, I would have to admit that I am not nearly as loving as I wish I were. What I am is polite. Sadly, there is a difference. Polite lets me keep my distance while performing all the pleasant rituals of a civilized society. Loving would mean I would have to curtail whatever forward momentum I was riding, like a dog running out its leash, and sit, quietly in service to whatever time or task was necessary to support someone else's needs.

That's the kind of shit that just ruins my to-do list—a list that, though it is a mile long and seems necessary to complete, I yearn to feed to a paper shredder the very second I complete it. Instead, I endow it with mythical importance while ironically using it to shield me from actual, authentic, and potentially significant interactions with actual, authentic, and definitely significant human beings.

"Too busy! Too busy!" I yell, waving my hands, metaphorically, in the air, "I can't possibly—I'm all booked up. I'm clearly important over here. Lots to do." After too long of this, it starts to sink into even my thick skull—none of the busy work we do to convince ourselves that we have purpose and drive is important. We mistake errands for meaning. Let me tell you, if I get to the end of my days and find out that, in fact, the meaning of life has anything to do with folding towels or cleaning the bathroom or multiple trips to the supermarket to ensure we never run out of vanilla soy milk, I am going to be super pissed. Someone is going to have to call the manager because I will want my money back.

Why do I fill up all my time with crap I do not care the slightest bit about? Do you know what I love? Movies. Do you know another thing I love? My kids. Do you know that I have a son who wants to become a movie director? Ask me how many movies we've been to together in the past year.

Zero.

You know what else I like to do? Art projects. I just finished a beautiful mosaic for the outside of our house. And to think, it only took me seventeen years to get around to it.

This bull-pucky has to stop. My time is 100 percent being eaten away by things that have nothing to do with me. Maybe that is where the rejection from my kids is coming from. When I ask my son, "Hey, do you want to run errands with me?" I get a resounding, "No." He's no dummy. No kid wants to trail behind his or her distracted, hurried mom, being urged to "Walk faster," because her brain is already thinking ahead to the next damn store she has to drive to and wondering if that vacuum repair place is open on Sundays.

"Do you want to help paint the garage?" No.

"Return these books to the library?" No.

"Go for a walk because vitamin D is good for us, especially in the winter?" No.

But, what if I said, "Hey, do you want to go to the new movie from our favorite director? Then afterwards, I will bribe you with ice cream and we can discuss how he chose to frame certain important shots and also the effectiveness of the score?"

He might still say no, unless I made it clear that I was paying, but there is a much greater chance that he might say yes because I was actually looking to share something of myself in the process. Plus, who doesn't love ice cream?

And what if I knocked on my daughter's door and said, "Do you want to come out to the dining room? I thought we could make seed art portraits of Grumpy Cat and enter them in this year's state fair."

Who am I kidding? She'd still probably elect to stay in her room. It's going to take more than a hilarious Internet meme to get her to voluntarily spend any time with her mother. I'd be out here, though. Just me taking the time to be me—and that would be a step in the right direction .

Secrets Parents Keep

One thing that other parents don't tell you is that your kids are going to hurt your feelings. Their disrespect and disobedience will make you feel, at times, like you are eight years old and someone on the playground just announced that you are fat and smell weird. (What? Just me?) You will feel isolated, alone, and entirely exposed to their ridicule because the thing you want more than anything else is their constant, unwavering love.

That in itself isn't so bad, but the other thing parents aren't going to tell you, because not one of us wants to admit it, is that sometimes, in that place of rejection and hurt, you are going to say something so intentionally mean to your precious child that the rest of the day, and possibly the week, will be spent in a state of hopeless regret. You will, in fact, never truly get over it and will turn it round and round in your mind in those late, vulnerable hours of the night when everything you have ever done comes back to punish you.

I, myself, am there right now. I also, just to cap off the experience, have emptied a generous slug of whiskey into my coffee, at nine fifteen in the morning.

Mother of the year, right here.

Kids are jerks. Did that sound harsh? It shouldn't because it's a solid fact. We all were jerks. Chief among our many transgressions was the stalwart refusal to see our parents as actual people with feelings or personal motivations akin to our own. To the child's eye, parents are automatons, programmed to dispense nutritional pellets in the form of PB&Js, apple slices, and cookies; to sign parental permission forms and bring new socks. No, not those socks, the anklet version. Black, not white! And not with seams on the toes!

I have been driven to despair by my children more times than I can count. Twice I felt so defeated that I was forced to lie, sobbing, *on the actual ground* because weeping in my chair did not adequately express the pain in my heart. At no other time in my life, not as a young child, not as a clearly misunderstood and underappreciated teenager, not as a struggling young wife was I ever so distraught. As a mother, the only thing I want is to do right by my kids, to raise them to feel strong and happy and safe and loved, always loved. Unfortunately, the little buggers make it so damn hard.

There are so many things nobody told me about being a parent. Things I might have surmised, if I were being a little more realistic about the whole thing. I guess in my mind's eye, I saw becoming a mother as a transformative experience. Inspired by my love for my offspring, I would become gentle, wise, and ever patient.

Do I need to tell you that is not what happened? Nope. I remained—me. But with a squalling youngster. I did not actually become the Mother Teresa/*Leave It to Beaver* mom I assumed would magically happen as soon as I was thrust into the role. Yes, I enjoy the crap out of my children, sometimes, but other times I just want to lie in bed, drinking coffee and reading in an entirely silent house—just like always. I find it extraordinarily hard to be ever-patient when I am smack dab in the middle of a project and I am inevitably interrupted by a slew of requests, nay, demands by the true lords and ladies of the house. I do not like anything I did not like before, and that includes playing with Legos, chicken nuggets, and children's sporting events.

Unfortunately, my preferences have little bearing on how I spend my days. Lately, I've been spending a lot of time at our city's baseball fields. Little Man is in full baseball season mode. It struck me last night that there was a marked difference between me and the rest of the parents littering the field. The majority of these folks have little kids, and their son or daughter out on the field may be the oldest or possibly their second child but certainly not their youngest. They spend their time chatting with each other, taking videos of their toddlers on their phones, comparing videos, setting up play dates, and being generally friendly and delightful. They are engaged in the game and full of energy.

I sit in my chair, bitterly resentful that I forgot a magazine and pondering how bad it would be if I brought a travel mug full of merlot to the park. I don't chat; I don't make friends. I count down the innings until I can get home and lie, face down on the couch, until it's time for bed. I am engaged with the game only in so much as I really, really want to know how long until it's over. Luckily after being through this with four other kids, I know that my son is not going to even be looking at me. He's hanging with his friends, perfecting the twin skills of pitching and spitting sunflower seed shells over the fence. All that is required is for me to aim my face in his general direction and try not to scowl while I do it.

Make no mistake, I am terribly proud of him. The only time I perk up at all is when he is up to bat or his best friend is in the batter's box. That kid I like. The rest of them? Meh.

So here's another secret for you. Just because you have kids doesn't mean you automatically like any other person's child. The idea that you will love all children once you have one is a crock of baloney or at least I hope it is. God, I'm going to feel like such a jerk if every other mother on the planet is truly as caring as I pretend to be. Fine, fine, children are the future and all that, but given the powerful biological urges that exist solely for the purpose of driving us to protect our children from harm and not, say, leave them in the grocery store parking lot every time they have a tantrum, I think it's clear that undying adoration for these demanding, unsocialized, unfiltered little animals is not quite as easy as it's chalked up to be. And why, given how very many grown-ups I find vexing, would I be expected to be fast friends with their offspring? Little children with which I am not even related? You must be joking.

And just in case you side-stepped that little land mine, there is a good chance that should you happen to like your child's friends, it won't even matter because your child will come to prefer to spend his or her time with some other family, not yours, so you will never see your own flesh and blood child. Today my eldest son called me, as he tends to do, and asked if he could go to a barbecue at a friend's house. Now, this is the child with the social life to rival a Kardashian. We never see the boy. He bops from work to sleepovers to picnics to barbecues. The majority of his friends have no siblings. Maybe one, at most. We get detailed and breathless reports of how large his friends' bedrooms are, how many snacks are in their pantry, how many cool gadgets they own. I suspect that when he hangs at their relatively quiet and spacious digs, he feels the relief of a circus performer, released from the oppressive confines of a clown car.

Not that I'm bitter.

Okay, maybe a little, but only because I would like to see him every now and again, you know? It is a terribly kept secret that I am jealous of all the time he spends with people who are not me.

I think he can hear the edge in my voice when he calls with these requests.

"What's wrong?" he asks.

"Nothing, " I sniff. "Have a good time."

Because what am I going to say? "I want you to *want* to hang with me?" That's the kind of thing you say to your college boyfriend, not your son, unless you want to be the kind of mother that ends up mummified and stuffed in the attic while the boy in question is downstairs, wearing your house dress, murdering unsuspecting co-eds in the shower. Or so I've been told.

No, thank you. So I told him to go, have fun, hang out with his friends and their families, and make sure to thank their mothers—even though they had absolutely nothing to do with making you or birthing you or protecting and nurturing and loving you, lo these many years. No, go, I'm sure they are *just great.*

Harrumph.

The thing is, I could totally see where he was coming from. I don't want to hang around this place either, and do you know why? Because we don't do anything fun, that's why. Because every minute that isn't consumed by actual gainful employment is spent working: laundry, dishes, sweeping, weeding. Blech. I hate all of it. And I'm the *grown-up* in this scenario.

So I came home, put away groceries, stomped downstairs to do some laundry, stomped back upstairs to clean the living room and start making lunches for the week, then suddenly, I stopped. Because here's the other thing, parents: The kids are fine. They are just as fine in a house with dirty dishes piled to the ceiling as they are in a home that sparkles. Furthermore, they have no *idea* how you spend your day. If you are lucky enough to have a moment to yourself, spending even a second of it on the soul-numbing errands you do every other day of the week is just plain foolish. The best thing for turning any of this around is a day spent doing none of this crap. Might I suggest a nap? Cookies for lunch? An afternoon spent watching movies on Netflix? In short, do anything that makes you feel like a sane and rational person again. And this isn't a secret, it's something we've all heard, something that we've counseled others about, but we have to take care of ourselves in order to joyfully and wholeheartedly take care of the little darlings. Those frustrating, delicious, maddening, precious darlings. So do whatever it is you need to do to set yourself right. And if that thing happens to look like a good, old-fashioned Irish coffee for breakfast, well, you know I won't judge.

Lessons for Mom

I've been sending a friend of mine chapters of this book, trusting her to ferret out errors in grammar, misspellings, and potential warning signs of a nervous breakdown. She's trying to read it objectively, as if she doesn't know me. Here's an excerpt from the feedback I got today: "I'm really excited to see what wisdom the character gains from this. What does she learn? How does she grow?"

I turned to Hubby and said, "I don't think it's that kind of book."

I guess in an ideal world it would be. Parenthood would lead to all sorts of personal breakthroughs and enlightenment bordering on the spiritual. Unfortunately, in my case, the only things it has led to is stress-induced weight gain and an alarming and overpowering urge to wear pajamas as clothing.

Her remark did get me thinking though—is there something I hope to learn from all this? Is there the potential to emerge, like a brilliant butterfly, from this domestic cocoon? This messy, sticky, noisy cocoon?

You know, there is a school of thought that believes everyone who comes into our lives is a teacher, here to bring us knowledge of what we most need to learn. If that is even remotely true, my greatest teacher of all has to be our youngest son. Little Man and I are most frequently at loggerheads. Many are the days that Hubby comes home and finds the two of us, nose to nose, neither one backing down an inch, each one convinced we could successfully make our point, if the other would just stop talking and *listen*, for one stupid, stinking minute.

It is a sad day when you figure that, yes, a ten-year-old *is* the boss of you.

I cannot even count the number of times I have mentally paused, mid-rant, and wondered just which one of us I am lecturing. It happens when I admonish him, saying, "You don't always need to have the last word." Or when I exclaim in exasperation, "You don't always need to be right, you know." I think it when I try to quell his fears, counseling, "You don't need to be so worried about what other people think about you." Or when I look him straight in the face, smooth his hair from his forehead, and say with all the sincerity and wisdom I can muster, "You are pushing back so hard right now because you are afraid that there is something wrong with you. You need to always remember, that even when you make mistakes, you are good and worthy and loved." At times like that, I half expect him to disappear in a puff of smoke, replaced by Clarence, the angel from *It's a Wonderful Life*, thanking me for the sudden revelation that allowed him to finally get his wings.

But, no. Apparently I am hopelessly clueless. Enlightenment just doesn't stick with me. Five minutes after what I could swear is a life-shattering breakthrough, I'm back to my oblivious, self-doubting ways. I blame the Internet. I'm more addicted to streaming *Real Housewives* than achieving any of my life's goals. It's such an unfair fight. Wrestle with insecurity or drink red wine and watch human car wrecks from the safety of my couch? Left to myself, there is definitely no contest. Human car wrecks all the way. But I have kids. And while I strongly suspect it is far too late for me, I wouldn't want them to follow those footsteps. I don't want them to interact with the world according to *my* all too blatant faults.

So I try to clean up my act. I put a smile on my face and head out running even when I want to sleep the extra hour because, look, kids, fitness is important. I stop myself after two glasses of wine because moderate drinking is healthy, but alcoholism is not. I do not lie on the couch sobbing when I don't get my way (no matter how much I'd like to) because that is not how we do things, children. If I want my kids to dust themselves off and try, try again, Mom needs to show it can be done.

In a real sense, I am acting exactly as I did when I was a kid. My mom used to leave an after-school chore list that needed to be done before she got home from work, you know, to add a little structure to our afternoons. And it worked because we had a definite routine down: Arrive home from school, toss book bags, coats, any which place. Commence eating contraband frozen Suzy Q snack cakes from Mom's stash in the freezer and watch *Little House on the Prairie*. Fight with siblings over television, eat more snack cakes. Call best friend on shared party-line landline phone, ignore five-minute phone conversation rules and endless clicking in of neighbors wishing to use phone (probably for work-related conversations or possibly to call for medical services). Watch more TV. Realize mom is due home in fifteen minutes. Panic. Scream at siblings that chores need to be done *now*. Forgo working cooperatively in favor of yelling curses and threats at each other while running around like lunatics. Hear Mom's car in the driveway. Grab random textbook and assume scholarly air of nonchalance.

"Mother, is that you? We didn't hear you come in."

Today is my day off. It looked like this: Put on running clothes. Arrange face in pleasant and vaguely athletic air of excitement. Wave good-bye to the children. Go for run. Return to an empty house. Watch crappy TV until chilled. Take shower. Make banana bread. Eat banana bread. Troll Facebook, gossip sites, etc. and eat more banana bread. Realize that somehow I have managed to laze away the entire day, consumed all of the sweet bread, and now the whole brood is due home in half an hour. Quickly start supper, completely trashing the kitchen in the process. Make the world's easiest chocolate cake. (It mixes in the pan and takes two minutes to assemble and slide into the oven. Really, this family will forgive anything if there is chocolate cake at the end.) Intone to incoming children that I am exhausted, *exhausted*, and sweetly ask them to clean the kitchen.

Oh, I am the worst. How I managed to get to this age and be so completely clueless is just beyond me. Case in point: I almost made a trip to the store the other day to purchase matcha green tea. I'd just read an Internet article on it that extolled the many antioxidants in it, the calm alertness it provides, the possible immunity boost. I had gone as far as collecting my coat and purse, when I remembered, I hate green tea. Blech. Hate it. It's weak and bitter and, like all tea, tastes disappointingly like grass water. Worst of all, it is not coffee. Coffee is delicious and complex and somehow thick. If coffee were people, it would wrap you in a blanket, throw an arm around you, and call you "friend." If tea were people, it would tell you to change clothes because it wanted to go to that organic sushi place downtown, the one where the air conditioning is always set too high and the portions are far too small. High expectations leading to disappointment, every single time.

So, given that I clearly have such strong opinions on the matter, why would I even consider bringing the stuff into my house? I'll tell you why; because I have always confused the person I want to be with the person I actually am. I am not an artist or a great philosopher; I have no natural tendencies toward tidiness or an innate talent for organization. I tend to sloth and comfort, and if I have a single superpower, it is that I can predict—to the exact dialogue about to be spoken—what is going to happen next in any given movie. (Except for those British tragedies. They set up such an ominous mood that I always overshoot the target. I'm like, "Incest! Buried alive! Sold for body parts!" and the only trauma the main character ends up wrestling with is losing his job and maybe not getting along with his oh so proper mother. Darn you, BBC. I will crack your code yet.)

This is the kind of misinterpretations that vex me as a mother, as well. How I long to be the elegant, unflappable sort of parent, the kind who moves with unshakeable ease through the unexpected maelstrom of life with demanding youngsters. You missed the bus and need a ride? No problem. You signed up to bring a dish for the PTA potluck this very evening? Easy peasy. Your debate tournament starts in an hour and you need me to run to school with a clean and pressed oxford shirt and your good shoes? I would adore doing this thing for you. Nothing would make me happier, my child.

Phfft. As if. In reality, if my kids so much as ask me to sign a permission slip after supper, my body goes weak and boneless and I slide to the floor, sobbing into the back of my arm, "Why, sweet Jesus, WHY?" I think I used up all my reserve of motherly calm maybe three years ago.

So what kind of mother am I? I am not a hovering mom, that's for sure. Yes, I fret and worry and wring my hands over threats to my children's well-being, real or imagined, the same as every other mom. I just prefer to do it from my couch and not in the classroom, a PTA meeting, or the doctor's office. My general rule is: I will help you with anything outside your ability, but if you are able to do it yourself, good luck and God bless.

I know other parents do it differently, mostly because I have been informed as such by the other children my kids bring into my home. Recently, I was told by one of them that they were "kind of bored" because there were "no activities planned." Never mind that the children involved are all middle-schoolers. Rather than respond in the same, vaguely accusatory tone that I was not accustomed to planning out play dates for *thirteen-year-olds*, I merely smiled, baked the pizza at the exact time she had instructed me to, and then set about plotting ways to ensure that this particular child would never darken our doorstep again.

A somewhat illuminating example, but it occurs to me that once again, I am defining myself as what I am not. Maybe the best lesson that I could hope for from parenthood is that it provides the exact, perfect hothouse scenario to figure out what I am.

I am in love with all my kids, though uncomfortably impatient when it comes down to it. I am eternally optimistic, to judge from the lists I make for myself each morning. I have an innate belief in my capacity to succeed in untested situations, although I'm loath to back up that belief with action. I'm restless with the desire to be "all in" but frightened to throw down. I have a protective reserve that I hope to God my kids feel that they can easily pierce. I am pig-headed but mature enough to say sorry, even to bossy ten-year-olds. I regret deeply the mistakes I've made and haven't forgiven myself for any of them. I limit my time with "outsiders" because I'm afraid they will come to expect something of me and I am terribly protective of the time I can call my own. This juggernaut of parenting is nothing less than a hall of mirrors. If I take the time and pause for just a moment, I may emerge having learned a tremendous amount about what I am and what I hope to be.

Well, I'll be darned. Maybe this *is* that kind of book, after all.

The Beginning of the End

So, it's come to this: Miss Teen Wonder is gone, lost to the college years. All the kids are older now. They are more independent and absorbed with, I don't know, whatever it is that teenagers do to amuse themselves these days.

Sometimes Hubby and I watch the neighbors across the street. Their kids are much younger than ours. When they arrive home from work, before they even have a chance to lock the car, the house door is flung violently open and their little linebacker of a son barrels down the sidewalk, yelling "Daddy!"or "Mommy!" his wee arms outstretched for a hug. Hubby and I will gaze at each other and smile softly, remembering the times our children did the same. Then I'll go inside and try to find a single one of the ingrates here who will agree to play cribbage with their mother.

No dice, old lady.

Hattie leaving for college was such a decisive moment for us. A year later and my internal history of our family still feels defined by the shift—Before Hattie Left and After She Was Gone. I'm tearing up now, just thinking about it, and the girl is currently home for the summer. She is at this moment sleeping on the basement couch. There appears a really good chance I may cry about this forever.

That last summer Before She Left, I thought, "Good Lord, get this child away from me." I would get together with my girlfriends who had children the same age and our stories were remarkably similar— ungrateful children apparently taken total leave of their senses and believing themselves to be exempt from all the longstanding rules of our families because they had graduated and were "all grown up." (Snort.) They were eating all the food, refusing to do dishes, running around with their friends every night, ignoring any requests to do their chores, and avoiding chatting with their families. To them, every night was special: The Last Time they would be together with their friends at the coffee shop or the movies. The Last Time they would see their best friend before she or he left. It was special, all right, a special pain in my butt.

Finally, the blessed day I was to drive Miss Teen Wonder to college arrived, and I promptly burst into tears. I cried for weeks after that, months really. I have never been so depressed in all my days. It caught everyone off guard, the way I would lie on the sofa, dripping silent tears, limp as a suicidal jellyfish. The most ridiculous aspect of the whole thing was that my daughter was going to school a mere half an hour away. She was literally a trip to the mall away from me, and I was acting as dramatic as Anna Karenina staring at the train tracks.

The amazing thing about social media is that it offers many new and innovative means of staying connected, but also twenty different ways to feel hopelessly rejected. I was trying mightily to respect my daughter's "space," the result being I felt exactly like a thirteen-year-old girl desperately in love with a boy who may, or may not, call. Except, this being the brave new world that it is, he isn't texting, Facebooking, Kik-ing, or Snapchatting either. It was a terrible time.

How ironic that the final stage of parenting depends solely on our absence, that the goal of the many years spent nurturing them, caring for them, and giving them all the tools to be self-reliant, competent adults is that, well, they become self-reliant and competent and, as a result, do not need us at all. This is not my favorite part of the plan. It feels like a sucker punch to the stomach.

Unbeknownst to me at the time, Miss Teen Wonder wasn't exactly having a wonderful time of it, either. It took many weeks before she called and admitted, her voice breaking on the phone line, that she was horribly, terribly homesick. We were quite the pair that night, both clutching our phones and wailing. And the worst, the absolute most unfair aspect of the whole situation, was that I couldn't do what I so desperately wanted to do, which was tell her to just come home, forget it, it's too hard.

Probably the greatest influence on shaping my own parenting philosophy, other than my actual parents, was an article I read once that said, basically, when you tell your child that, no, there are no monsters under the bed, you do not then drop to your knees to check. Doing so negates anything that you have just said and plants the suspicion in your child's mind that your word is not necessarily reliable. So, when my precious daughter called me, crying, scared, and lonely, I could not drop to my knees and look for boogie men. I had to repeat what I had always maintained—you are smart; you are capable; you are talented and lovable. You do not need me to save you from what is scary in this world. When times are hard, you are strong enough to find your way, and I absolutely couldn't be prouder.

I do not understand how I was not immediately handed a medal for such an unselfish and difficult act. Clearly the Parent of the Year committee should have been contacted when I did not swoop into her dorm and collect her, as much as I wanted to. I did, however, stop acting like a jilted middle-schooler and started sending my own, more frequent texts and messages to serve as little signs of support from home. They were nothing poetic or inspirational. We tend to communicate largely in hilarious cat videos and terrible puns, but I hope the message is clear: "I love you. I miss you. I am so proud— also, katz! Am I right?"

Maybe it worked because she started to get her footing the second half of the year. She made some truly wonderful friends and settled into life in the dorms, rife with all the drama hormonally charged nineteen-year-olds tend to bring. She joined the Feminist Club and spent a week hiking in the North Woods with her friends. She signed up for a semester studying abroad. She seemed finally ready to officially leave the nest. I was delighted.

And yet . . .

Last night I had a terrible dream. I dreamt that Hubby was a chef/chiropractor, which seemed perfectly logical at the time. A rival chef/chiropractor at first attempted to discredit him and, when that didn't work, set out to murder our entire family. Somehow, as we were fleeing to safety, I was driving alone and became separated from the rest of our group. Miss Teen Wonder came back for me. But it wasn't my grown child. It was her at the age of seven. Exactly. Same pig tails, same lopsided dimple, riding up to find me on her slightly too large pink bicycle.

I think even in my dream, I gasped when I saw her. My baby. The sense of loss, of having missed this child, was so deep that I couldn't breathe. Yet, there was no time to waste. I couldn't leave my vehicle to embrace her, to kiss her sweet cheeks, or smell the top of her head.

"We have to *go!*" I urgently called, but she wouldn't be rushed. She pedaled off to the side of the road and, with a flourish, whisked out a gold, sequined cape. Only after she had secured it around her neck would she start out.

From my higher vantage point, I could see cars closing in on us, but where I saw peril, she saw only adventure. I could not, from my car, alert her to the dangers ahead. I could only watch, helplessly, as she pedaled furiously, loving the feeling of forward motion, grinning into the wind.